D0401100

PENGUIN BOOKS

THE MEASURE OF MY DAYS

Florida Pier Scott-Maxwell was born in Orange Park, Florida, on September 24, 1883. She had lessons at home until she was ten, briefly attended public school in Pittsburgh, then went back to private lessons, and finally gave it all up to go on the stage at sixteen. At twenty she abandoned that career and began another as a writer of short stories. In 1910 she married John Maxwell Scott-Maxwell and went to live in his native Scotland. Until 1935 she worked for women's suffrage, wrote plays, and tended her flowers and children. Among her books are *Towards Relationships* (1939), *Women and Sometimes Men* (1957), and the plays *The Flash-point* (1914), *They Know How to Die* (1931), and *Many Women* (1933). In 1933 Florida Scott-Maxwell trained for still another career as an analytical psychologist, studying under Carl Jung. She practiced in psychology clinics in Scotland and England. Florida Scott-Maxwell died in 1979.

FLORIDA SCOTT-MAXWELL

THE MEASURE
    OF MY DAYS

PENGUIN BOOKS

PENGUIN BOOKS
Published by the Penguin Group
Penguin Group (USA) Inc., 375 Hudson Street, New York, New York 10014, U.S.A.
Penguin Books Ltd, 80 Strand, London WC2R 0RL, England
Penguin Books Australia Ltd, 250 Camberwell Road, Camberwell, Victoria 3124, Australia
Penguin Books Canada Ltd, 10 Alcorn Avenue, Toronto, Ontario, Canada M4V 3B2
Penguin Books India (P) Ltd, 11 Community Centre, Panchsheel Park, New Delhi – 110 017, India
Penguin Books (N.Z.) Ltd, Cnr Rosedale and Airborne Roads, Albany, Auckland, New Zealand
Penguin Books (South Africa) (Pty) Ltd, 24 Sturdee Avenue,
Rosebank, Johannesburg 2196, South Africa

Penguin Books Ltd, Registered Offices: 80 Strand, London WC2R 0RL, England

First published in the United States of America by
Alfred A. Knopf, Inc., 1968
Published in Penguin Books 1979

30 29 28

LIBRARY OF CONGRESS CATALOGING IN PUBLICATION DATA:
Scott-Maxwell, Florida Pier, 1883–1979
The measure of my days.
Reprint of the 1st ed. published in 1968 by
Knopf, New York.
I. Old age.   2. Aged women—United States—Biography.   I. Title.
[HQ1061.S36   1979]   301.43′5′0924   78–27682
ISBN 0 14 00.5164 3

Printed in the United States of America
Set in Monotype Bell

THE MEASURE OF MY DAYS

We who are old know that age is more than a disability. It is an intense and varied experience, almost beyond our capacity at times, but something to be carried high. If it is a long defeat it is also a victory, meaningful for the initiates of time, if not for those who have come less far.

Being old I am out of step, troubled by my lack of concord, unable to like or understand much that I see. Feeling at variance with the times must be the essence of age, and it is confusing, wounding. I feel exposed, bereft of a right matrix, with the present crime, violence, nihilism heavy on my heart. I weigh and appraise, recoiling, suffering, but very alert. Now that I have withdrawn from the active world I am more alert to it than ever before. Old people have so little personal life that the impact of the impersonal is sharp. Some of us feel like sounding boards, observing, reading; the outside event startles us and we ask in alarm, "Is this good or bad? To where will it lead? What effect will it have on people, just people? How different will they become?" I fear for the future.

In the past when sorrows, or problems, or ideas were too much for me, I learned to deal with them in a way of my own. At night when I got to bed I lay on my back and gave to their solution what I knew would be many sleepless hours. I would let the problem enter me like a lance piercing my solar plexus. I must be open, utterly open, and as I could stand it the lance went deeper and deeper. As I accepted each implication, opened to my hurt, my protest, resentment and bewilderment the lance went further in. Then the same for others involved—that they did, said, felt, thus and so, then why, face why and endure the lance. As my understanding deepened I could finally accept the truths that lay behind the first truths that had seemed unendurable. At last, the pain of the lance was not there and I was free. No, free is not the right word. My barriers had been lowered and I knew what I had not known before.

Now that I am old something has begun that is slightly the same, enough the same to make me start this note book. When I was sewing, or playing a soothing-boring game of patience, I found queries going round and round in my head and I began to jot them down in this note book which I used to use for sketching. The queries were insistent, and I began a game of asking questions and giving answers. Answers out of what I had read and forgotten, and now thought my own, or out of my recoils and hopes. If the modern world is this, then will it become so and so? My answers must be my own, years of reading now lost in the abyss I call my mind. What matters is what I have now, what in fact I live and feel.

It makes my note book my dear companion, or my undoing. I put down my sweeping opinions, prejudices, limitations, and just here the book fails me for it makes no comment. It is even my wailing wall, and when I play that grim, comforting game of noting how wrong everyone else is, my book is silent, and I listen to the stillness, and I learn.

I am getting fine and supple from the mistakes I've made, but I wish a note book could laugh. Old and alone one lives at such a high moral level. One is surrounded by eternal verities, noble austerities to scale on every side, and frightening depths of insight. It is inhuman. I long to laugh. I want to be enjoyed, but an hour's talk and I am exhausted.

What a time of fact finding this is. Research into everything, committees of experts formed to solve each problem that arises; computers given

The Measure of My Days

more information than would seem possible for a human brain to use, and statistics taken as final truth. The stir and determination make it appear that the complexities of life have just been noticed, but soon every detail will be clearly seen and solved.

Yet something very different seems the taste of the age, a liking for the blurred, the unlabelled, amounting to a preference for sameness, inclusion, oneness. To include and condone is modern, while to differentiate is old fashioned. This seems to hold socially, morally. Is it a claim that the less good is not exactly the same as the good, yet it has its rights, and must be protected as though it contained a new value? Perhaps it does. New values are coming to birth and suspension of judgment may be wise. Or are we all so confused that we remain amorphous, hoping a new pattern will form itself without our help?

There seems a widespread need of living and learning the dark side of our nature. Perhaps we are almost on the point of saying that evil is normal, in each of us, an integral part of our being. This age may be witnessing the assimilation of evil, thereby finding a new wisdom. We have been insisting for centuries that evil should not be, that it can be eliminated, is only the absence of good, resides in others; if others are evil we are not, or so little that it hardly matters. Now we are fascinated by evil. Does it begin to be clear that it is half of life, and at its extreme is truly evil? Are we learning that without the tension between good and evil there would be no dynamism in life? Perhaps our two cruel wars were a climax of evil making us see a truth we have always fled; if this profound realisation is taking place, then what seems our decadence may be the stirring of a new reality, even a new morality, God willing and man able.

What a perilous morality. Will humanity ever be equal to it? Where will the difference lie between the man who blindly lives his chaos, and the man who consciously endures the conflict between the opposing sides of his nature? The latter will gain clarity, a deepened awareness, and he will achieve responsibility for many aspects of his being, but much of the time the two men will look the same.

I notice that parents are very cautious about inculcating any special virtues in their young. They almost look to the young to create whatever virtue they need most. This behaviour can seem a failure, a wrong done to the young, but parents may be mute because they are unsure, and so the young are forced to choose, to learn the reality of good and evil at first hand. All this may have to be. Adults are bankrupt of certitudes. The young may have to learn in their own right the negative of every positive. That evil is the inevitable half of good may be the unacceptable truth that we are all taking in, and it could be the forerunner of a new balance. If such a possibility lies ahead, then we must be moving toward a goal of greater consciousness, where we will admit our dual natures, and assume responsibility for all that lies within us.

Has this hope not lain behind all moral effort, all the varying attempts that brought such bad with such good? Have we come anywhere near the avowal, "Evil that belongs to me is my sacred responsibility?" Or are we only saying— "Evil hardly matters, we like it." What confusion we are in, and what soil for new virtues. May the young be strong. We have to hope, for our present formlessness could lead to self-hatred. It might even lead to a hatred of others, which could create a wish for destruction, until atomic war could express humanity's verdict on itself. This is too dreadful to look at. Do old people see life in terms of failure because we are failing? Perhaps. We are apocalyptic. We no longer function, so we warn and condemn. The only useful thing we might do is to feel compassion for those who make the mistakes we are too old to make.

I used to draw, absorbed in the shapes of roots of trees, and seed pods, and flowers, but it strained my eyes and I gave it up. Then ten years ago I began to make rugs. A few were beautiful, though never straight. This gave them vitality. As I created patterns, banged and pulled, the wool and I struggling—the wool winning sometimes; at great moments I in full command—my heart knew peace, and my mind was as empty as a cloudless sky on a summer's day. But my hands were too arthritic, it had to end, and now only music prevents my facing my thoughts.

Age puzzles me. I thought it was a quiet time. My seventies were interesting, and fairly serene, but my eighties are passionate. I grow more intense as I age. To my own surprise I burst out with hot conviction. Only a few years ago I enjoyed my tranquillity; now I am so disturbed by the outer world and by human quality in general that I want to put things right, as though I still owed a debt to life. I must calm down. I am far too frail to indulge in moral fervour.

Old people are not protected from life by engagements, or pleasures, or duties; we are open to our own sentience; we cannot get away from it, and it is too much. We should ward off the problematic, and above all the insoluble. These are far, far too much, but it is just these that attract us. Our one safety is to draw in, and enjoy the simple and immediate. We should rest within our own confines. It may be dull, restricted, but it can be satisfying within our own walls. I feel most real when alone, even most alive when alone. Better to say that the liveliness of companionship and the liveliness of solitude differ, and the latter is never as exhausting as the former. When I am with other people I try to find them, or try to find a point in myself from which to make a bridge to them, or I walk on the egg-shells of affection trying not to hurt or misjudge. All this is very tiring, but love at any age takes everything you've got.

What fun it is to generalize in the privacy of a note book. It is as I imagine waltzing on ice might be. A great delicious sweep in one direction, taking you your full strength, and then with no trouble at all, an equally delicious sweep in the opposite direction. My note book does not help me think, but it eases my crabbed heart.

I love my family for many reasons; for what I see them to be, for the loveliness they have been, for the good I know in them. I love their essence, their "could be", and all this in spite of knowing their faults well. I love the individual life in them that I saw when in bud. I have spent much of my life watching it unfold, enchanted and anxious.

The Measure of My Days

At times it has seemed like frail craft shaking out sails. I have feared for it when it was becalmed, when it was in danger, and when I knew nothing, nothing. I have felt respect, even reverence, for I have seen it meet tragedy and gain nobility. I have watched it win its prizes and I have learned the hard truth a mother learns slowly, that the quick of intimacy she has known becomes hope for loved strangers.

A mother's love for her children, even her inability to let them be, is because she is under a painful law that the life that passed through her must be brought to fruition. Even when she swallows it whole she is only acting like any frightened mother cat eating its young to keep it safe. It is not easy to give closeness and freedom, safety plus danger.

No matter how old a mother is she watches her middle-aged children for signs of improvement. It could not be otherwise for she is impelled to know that the seeds of value sown in her have been winnowed. She never outgrows the burden of love, and to the end she carries the weight of hope for those she bore. Oddly, very oddly, she is forever surprised and even faintly wronged that her sons and daughters are just people, for many mothers hope and half expect that their new-born child will make the world better, will somehow be a redeemer. Perhaps they are right, and they can believe that the rare quality they glimpsed in the child is active in the burdened adult.

Age is truly a time of heroic helplessness. One is confronted by one's own incorrigibility. I am always saying to myself, "Look at you, and after a lifetime of trying." I still have the vices that I have known and struggled with—well it seems like since birth. Many of them are modified, but not much. I can neither order nor command the hubbub of my mind. Or is it my nervous sensibility? This is not the effect of age; age only defines one's boundaries. Life has changed me greatly, it has improved me greatly, but it has also left me practically the same. I cannot spell, I am over critical, egocentric and vulnerable. I cannot be simple. In my effort to be clear I become complicated. I know my faults so well that I pay them small heed. They are stronger than I am. They are me.

But who is it that knows me so well and has to endure me? There is the I that has to bear all the other I's and can assess them correctly; and there is the I who feels such sick distaste and drunken elation at being itself, all its selves, who is even thankful for the opportunity of having been itself, uncomfortable as it has been. Is the judging I a separate entity, and who can this wise I be? It feels higher, greater than I. I fail it, it scorns and rebukes me. Then who is it? I feel like a hierarchy, and perhaps I am one. I am my chief interest because to me I am life. My curiosity, delight, pain tell me about life itself. This makes me a monster of egotism, but that is what I am and have to be, for how else do I know, really know anything? I observe others, but I experience myself. As I long to understand, even a little, who could be as helpful to me as myself, muddled creature that I am, since it is my mortification, my respect that tells me what is real.

If I am myself with ardour, and no other way seems possible, I am also helpless in my own grasp. I come up against my own limitations as against granite. I observe and reflect yet when I am asked for an opinion I feel part of a network, am not a solid point, am very nearly absent. It amounts to this: that near the end of my life when I am myself as never before, I am awareness at the mercy of multiplicity. Ideas drift in like bright clouds, arresting, momentary, but they come as visitors. A shaft of insight can enter the back of my mind and when I turn to greet it, it is gone. I did not have it, it had me. My mood is light and dancing, or it is leaden. It is not I who choose my moods; I accept them, but from whom?

As I do not live in an age when rustling black silk skirts billow about me, and I do not carry an ebony stick to strike the floor in sharp rebuke, as this is denied me, I rap out a sentence in my note book and feel better. If a grandmother wants to put her foot down, the only safe place to do it these days is in a note book.

I suppose that humanity is still very tribal. It feels tribal. For centuries to come, perhaps forever we will be working out the separation of the individual from the collective bond—that protective oneness that you see everywhere, and know is deeply essential to each of us. Perhaps primitives are less closely held together than I assume, but their unchanging ways over long periods must imply the existence of very few people individual enough to differ from the group, or strong enough to establish their difference. Perhaps many do differ but wisely conceal it, since it is

The Measure of My Days

the most uncomfortable thing in the world to stand alone.

The ordeal of being true to your own inner way must stand high in the list of ordeals. It is like being in the power of someone you cannot reach, know, or move, but who never lets you go; who both insists that you accept yourself and who seems to know who you are. It is awful to have to be yourself. If you do reach this stage of life you are to some extent free from your fellows. But the travail of it. Precious beyond valuing as the individual is, his fate is feared and avoided. Many do have to endure a minute degree of uniqueness, just enough to make them slightly immune from the infection of the crowd, but natural people avoid it. They obey for comfort's sake the instinct that warns, "Say yes, don't differ, it's not safe". It is not easy to be sure that being yourself is worth the trouble, but we do know it is our sacred duty.

Perhaps these times in which we live are more dangerous than they seem, and in a different way. Mass values prevail until I wonder if we

are all herding together because a great challenge
lies ahead. If we can manage to face it an increase in consciousness could be due. Then who
is in greatest danger? Is it the individual whose
fate it is to oppose the mass, succour the nascent
value? The individual is the carrier of value by
which we live; but what if we forget this, what if
the crowd becomes too strong, what happens
then? Can the hero, the ordinary man of course,
rise to the height that will be required of him?

A man once said to me, "I don't mind your telling
me my faults, they're stale, but don't tell me my
virtues. When you tell me what I could be it
terrifies me." I was surprised then, I understand
now, because I believe we may be faced by the
need of living our strengths.

If truth is measured by numbers, it being assumed
that what the majority want is good and must be,
then my wild heart (my now wild heart that

never used to be wild—or if it was did not know it—did not indeed benefit by it) flames for the truth of the few. We choose many things by a tribal truth, many more than we like, but there is a truth in the very pit of one's being that opposes tribal good. What honest heart denies that many delights are based on the premise that others will not, even cannot, do what you do? Sometimes It Is because you feel the need of doing something in your own way, sometimes it is the sheer delight of being lawless that you crave; or, more lightly, because you are drawn to the charm of the exceptional. If too many do what you do its quality is changed. If some things are done commonly it becomes tasteless; but there are things that can be done rarely and remain delicious.

It is clearly innocent to wish to be quiet or alone, but then others must not come where you are. It is natural to wish to be the only one to leave your footprint on pristine sand; to lie in an unvisited wood is idyllic, but if others do the same then all is degraded. Even motoring, as it once was, required an almost empty road, and

24

The Measure of My Days

what sort of climber likes a crowded mountain peak? It is undeniable that one needs the absence of others to enjoy the magic of many things. I deny that these are privilege. They are necessities that man may know himself, and that man may know nature when she is unsullied by him. So vital are these joys that I am convinced that crowds endanger our quality; with them, in them, we become unworthy of each other. And what do we live by and for but that evanescent achievement, the merit of mankind?

How understandable that most of our beliefs protect us from the danger of being an individual. "Think of others" we were once taught. "Adapt, adapt" we are now told. But it is a coward cry, for he who after cruel buffeting wins to aloneness learns that life is a tragic mystery. We are pierced and driven by laws we only half understand, we find that the lesson we learn again and again is that of accepting heroic helplessness.

The Measure of My Days

Some uncomprehended law holds us at a point of contradiction where we have no choice, where we do not like that which we love, where good and bad are inseparable partners impossible to tell apart, and where we—heart-broken and ecstatic, can only resolve the conflict by blindly taking it into our hearts. This used to be called being in the hands of God. Has anyone any better words to describe it?

The opposition between the individual and the mass must be the very ground of evolution. The individual pushing his way forward, blind with insight, glad to face any risk at all. If the mass was a whit less leaden what a danger the individual could be. The individual afire with untested creativity, the mass the weight that tests the strongest. No wonder hate is engendered here.

It is better not to look for love's part in case love proves to be only the relief of losing oneself in a crowd of two. But hate comes with disagreement. If you are said to be in the wrong, then you are convinced a wrong has been done you, and you must fight in self-defence; for to be wrong in the eyes of others feels as though you had been destroyed. To test truth here could be the death of the collective man in you, so it could also be the point at which you found yourself. This must be the fear that is the first food of hate. The fear of discovering who you are, of putting your uniqueness to the test.

Must each of us come out of the crowd, the crowd in us, stand opposed, risk existence or non-existence, apart from the mass? What birth is as painful as this, a birth that may be a death, but may also be one's holy gift to one's fellows.

There is a special hate threatening now, when a sameness is being enforced on us, and we feel the impulse to fight for our difference. Should we fight this impulse and find a way of conforming, or should we fight all the rest in a refusal to conform? We are basically much the same, we need to feel with others. Yet it must be the very pulse of life that makes each mount on the shoulder of the next, trampling on those who would trample on him, forcing them below, for how can anyone be above if others are not below? Must one lose face, gain status, test oneself, measure oneself— is all this the rudimentary stage of becoming an individual, and is it the price paid for having left the safety of the crowd?

Fool that I am, I worry at the combat of life like a dog with an old shoe. It is differentiation in action, it is what the competitive nature of man forces him to do whether he will or no. It is the creation of quality, good and bad. Most women only half understand it and they tend to dislike it, for they feel the human price is too high. It is high. Good may lose and bad may win. The public view and the private differ. It could make unexpected history if wives wrote what they saw work—its efforts and its achievements—doing to their husbands; telling honestly how much of the husband is left for human purposes and how good the human quality remains.

My kitchen linoleum is so black and shiny that I waltz while I wait for the kettle to boil. This pleasure is for the old who live alone. The others must vanish into their expected role.

All those who through history have helped life to enlarge, to diversify—at their peril, always at their peril—have been strongly individual; above all the greatest, who was more than man. If more and more of us accept the task of living our individual fate, if we accept being woman, man, withdrawn or all-managing, of this race or that, and make of it completeness, encompassing all the nobilities and humiliations of which we alone are capable, then what self-respect we could develop, what cause we could have for paying respect to one another, to exchange courtesy and compassion. It must have been just this slow development of honour and humility that has given us, through time, the heart to go on. Perhaps many think that life is so difficult that we could not do more than we are doing, and they would scorn me as someone who bewails human quality.

They could be right. I dislike much in myself, and much in humanity, and believe half of life, a constantly shifting half, to warrant dislike. But if life is the tension between the opposites and has to be just as it is, I still marvel that it has to be quite so bad. But I judge what I half create, for it is my eyes and my tastes that make my world. It is my creation and concept that I have to inhabit. Here, just here, is the price of individuality. I assume that I made my world out of what life offered, but my innate quality must have drawn it towards me. I fused it all together only half knowing what I did. What felt at moments like the white heat of necessity was much my own doing, and it may have been a wrongheaded effort. I shall never know. No one can enter my world, nor can I enter the world of those I know best; we can pay visits in the entrance hall, and keep our eyes unfocussed. We can exchange gifts. Oh we can do that. We can offer our flowers of humility, appreciation and need, only asking that a meeting ground (that precious place) be kept open.

I used to find it difficult to talk to people newly met. Speech felt precipitate. A silent knowing should come first, sitting, smiling, holding hands, dancing perhaps without words, but talking is too committal for a beginning. I had one friend who always carried some small objects of interest in his pocket, and on occasion would show them; the skull of an asp, seed pods of rare shape. These made speech easy.

Another day to be filled, to be lived silently, watching the sky and the lights on the wall. No one will come probably. I have no duties except to myself. That is not true. I have a duty to all who care for me—not to be a problem, not to be a burden. I must carry my age lightly for all our sakes, and thank God I still can. Oh that I may to the end. Each day then, must be filled with my first duty, I must be "all right". But is this assurance not the gift we all give to each other daily, hourly?

I wonder if we need be quite so dutiful. With one friend of my own age we cheerfully exchange the worst symptoms, and our black dreads as well. We frequently talk of death, for we are very alert to the experience of the unknown that may be so near and it is only to those of one's own age that one can speak frankly. Talking of one's health, which one wants to do, is generally full of risks. Ill health is unpleasant to most healthy people as it makes them feel helpless, threatened, and it can feel like an unjustified demand for sympathy. Few believe in the pains of another, and if the person in pain has nothing to show, can forget the pain when interested, then where is the reality of it? In one's self, where it ought to be kept I suppose. Disabilities crowd in on the old; real pain is there, and if we have to be falsely cheerful, it is part of our isolation.

Another secret we carry is that though drab outside—wreckage to the eye, mirrors a mortification—inside we flame with a wild life that is almost incommunicable. In silent, hot rebellion we cry silently—"I have lived my life haven't I? What more is expected of me?" Have we got to pretend out of noblesse oblige that age is nothing, in order to encourage the others? This we do with a certain haughtiness, realising now that we have reached the place beyond resignation, a place I had no idea existed until I had arrived here.

It is a place of fierce energy. Perhaps passion would be a better word than energy, for the sad fact is this vivid life cannot be used. If I try to transpose it into action I am soon spent. It has to be accepted as passionate life, perhaps the life I never lived, never guessed I had it in me to live. It feels other and more than that. It feels like the far side of precept and aim. It is just life, the natural intensity of life, and when old we have it for our reward and undoing. It can—at moments—feel as though we had it for our glory. Some of it must go beyond good and bad, for at times—though this comes rarely, unexpectedly —it is a swelling clarity as though all was resolved. It has no content, it seems to expand us, it does not derive from the body, and then it is gone. It may be a degree of consciousness which lies outside activity, and which when young we are too busy to experience.

I wonder if living alone makes one more alive. No precious energy goes in disagreement or compromise. No need to augment others, there is just yourself, just truth—a morsel—and you. You went through those long years when it was pain to be alone, now you have come out on the good side of that severe discipline. Alone you have your own way all day long, and you become very natural. Perhaps this naturalness extends into heights and depths, going further than we know; as we cannot voice it we must just treasure it as the life that enriches our days.

Impossible to speak the truth until you have contradicted yourself. Although I am absorbed in myself, a large part of me is constantly occupied with other people. I carry the thought of some almost as a baby too poorly to be laid down. There are many whom I never cease cherishing. I dwell on their troubles, their qualities, their possibilities as though I kept them safe by so doing; as though by understanding them I simplified their lives for them. I live with them every minute. I live by living with them. I dwell with the essence of friends so intensely that when they arrive I can be paralysed by the astonishing opacity of their actual presence.

We old *people* are short tempered because we suffer so. We are stretched too far, our gamut is painfully wide. Little things have become big; nothing in us works well, our bodies have become unreliable. We have to make an effort to do the simplest things. We urge now this, now that part of our flagging bodies, and when we have spurred them to further functioning we feel clever and carefree. We stretch from such concerns as these into eternity where we keep one eye on death, certain of continuity, then uncertain, then indifferent.

We cannot read the papers with the response of those younger. We watch the playing for place in great issues, we hear war rumble, and we who have lived long still feel the wounds of two wars endured. We remember the cost; the difference in mood at the beginning of a war and at the end of a war. The initial pride that forbids man to accept an affront and later, when the immeasurable has been accepted by all, the dumb sense of wrong done by all to all. So the old are past comment and almost past reaction, still knowing pity, but outside hope; also knowing—Oh here is the thing we cannot face again—that when man is set on a goal, destruction is nothing to him.

When a new disability arrives I look about to see if death has come, and I call quietly, "Death, is that you? Are you there?". So far the disability has answered, "Don't be silly, it's me."

The crucial task of age is balance, a veritable tightrope of balance; keeping just well enough, just brave enough, just gay and interested and starkly honest enough to remain a sentient human being. On the day when we can boast none of this, we must be able to wait until the balance is restored. When we sink to nothingness we must remember that only yesterday our love was warm. I believe, indeed I know, that for some people life lights a flame on the right shoulder, an accolade that may be for courage shown; when you are young the flame can leap because there is much life to be lived, and much need of fortitude. It can only burn faintly in age, but it may still be there. The old can supply little ardour, just the small amount we manage to create each day by our careful balancing. The flame may be unsteady but it can be clear, for it is still the greatness of being alive.

I must be explicit. The first dream I took to an analyst, many years ago, showed the three tall windows of his consulting room, windows almost from ceiling to floor. Outside them cosmic light streamed down. As this light is known, but no one knows what it is, there is no true name to give it. It is opaque light, very alive, moving, overpowering, and sparkling like a juicy apple when you bite deep.

It flowed down past the windows and I stood naked, barely able to endure the marvel. Then as

I sought shelter in the embrasure between two of the windows a small flame sprang to life on my right shoulder, and I knew it was an accolade.

If that happened to me, it has happened to others, and I take it as a fact of human experience.

In the landscape of the impersonal there is always the loved individual. The individual is there and loved, but this may sharpen the pain for the old. It is the long stretch of time that gives us our viewpoint. We have watched generation follow generation, and we see the same qualities in grandparents, parents, and children working the same sad havoc. We saw the same wounds we see now caused in a like manner long ago. We would like to warn and teach, but we have learned that it is almost useless. In the course of our lives we have amassed too much data for sharp sorrow; and if we have just as much reason for pity to have dulled, who wants pity? So how carry it?

Always, through everything, I try to straighten my spine, or my soul. They both ought to be upright I feel, for pride, for style, for reality's sake, but both tend to bend as under a weight that has been carried a long time. I try to lighten my burden by knowing it, I try to walk lightly, and sometimes I do, for sometimes I feel both light and proud. At other times I am bent, bent.

This morning when I woke and knew that I had had a fair night, that my pains were not too bad, I lay waiting for the uplifting moment when I pull back the curtains, see the sky, and I surprised myself by saying out loud: "My dear, dear days."

Personal immortality may not matter at all. Perhaps our long insistence on it has been our need of spiritual value, and a groping conviction that this is our central truth; that we have a share in impersonal greatness. We belie it daily, but is it not possible that by living our lives we create something fit to add to the store from which we came? Our whole duty may be to clarify and increase what we are, to make our consciousness a finer quality. The effort of one's entire life would be needed if we are to return laden to our source.

We may well fear that we will bring too small a gift, that we garner little. But are we fit judges, and out of travail and ignorance and loss, may we not create a kernel of gold that we dare not know, but which will be claimed?

I must ask myself, "What have I to become immortal? Not my beloved ego, none of that. And the spirit in us that is truly there, is that not already immortal?" Some rare people may have a special role to play, and they may remain themselves after death, but how worthy of immortality are most of us? We have to believe we have value, we could not have courage otherwise, and our sense of being more than ourselves is our most precious possession. It is in honour of this feeling that we endure and try. Even the most meagre life will have a wealth of patience, a treasure of endurance, immeasurable courage and cheer, and kindness culled from laborious days, and these are surely gifts worthy of return.

Age is a desert of time—hours, days, weeks, years perhaps—with little to do. So one has ample time to face everything one has had, been, done; gather them all in: the things that came from outside, and those from inside. We have time at last to make them truly ours.

When I was a child I went with my grandfather when he hunted wild turkey, or quail, driving through the roadless woods under great water oaks shining as though newly washed by rain. Once on reaching a river I jumped from the waggon and running into the deep shade sat down on a large alligator, taking it for a half-buried log. I was also the child who walked out on a plank placed as a pier to reach the centre of the dark pool, then knelt, plunged in her hands to scoop up a drink, and saw that fatal snake, a water moccasin, dart between her closing hands.

You need only claim the events of your life to make yourself yours. When you truly possess all you have been and done, which may take some time, you are fierce with reality. When at last age has assembled you together, will it not be easy to let it all go, lived, balanced, over?

Love opens double gates on suffering. The pain of losing good is the measure of its goodness. Parting is impoverishment. Reason gives no solace. The going away of someone loved is laceration. But courage, love, understanding, pity, sensitivity, all our glories almost break us. Then suffer. It is all I can do. But how carry it? Do not complain, much worse might come so easily. But I cannot just suffer, so I grope for a way of dealing with it, wondering how best to grasp it, searching for any insight that might help.

I know that bad as it seems for me, no good in it for me at all, the parting will bring new interest to those I am losing. I can do nothing—love and suffering are the same.

When I have looked at every side sorrow begins to be sorrow for the inscrutable sorrow of life. I sorrow over distance, just distance, with its power of annulling those far away. If I could only see far ahead, assess what will happen, but I can do nothing. So I ape a false cheer, and gradually my sorrow becomes a dumb facing of Fate, until sickened by acceptance I feel a change taking place. A hint comes of some melting or hardening—which is it?—and at last I reach an inner citadel where there is a wounded quiet, knowing strength.

Have I only given up protest and comment because I could not do less, or other? In that inner place, indefinable, but not an illusion, do I just capitulate? This may be so, must be so, but it feels otherwise. Perhaps near the core of our being—are we ever near that unknowable centre? —one is beyond pain and pleasure. Is it possible that we approach the place where they are one? Is this to say—"Thy will be done"?

Our sorrow is such a burden for others. If it were possible it might be best to show nothing, and this is often tried with arid results, for it is unreal, inhuman. You express some of your unhappiness, partly to rid yourself of a little, and partly because honesty itself demands some expression. Expressing sorrow helps you to take it in, to know it better. But soon, soon you must claim it as your own, relieving others of its weight, so that they can say happily, "Better today? All right now?" It is what they need to say, and you must answer brightly, "All right, thank you."

Dr. Johnson said that telling one's troubles was asking for pity or praise. Very good. You often need and deserve both pity and praise. Perhaps you need to share your weakness. That too is likely. But it is more than that. You ask to be met at the point of your reality.

When you have to accept loss, you know you are retreating on to less and less territory. The play of your heart will be restricted, the area of your interest lessened. The territory of the old is very small, and it hurts to diminish. When you reach this mute place you have no need to speak. It is no longer possible; and because you are cornered you are somehow saved. It is again the inner citadel, and unable to state it, incapable of in any way describing it, you only know that there in that one place is the relief of quiet.

The equal-ended cross surrounded by a circle, a pattern found in many countries, is taken as the oldest symbol of completeness, of integration. Our consciousness splits life into qualities, and so we know the tension of opposites, the basic differentiation. But the opposites are also the cross and you; if steadfast enough we may feel the stillness at the centre, and if acceptance is possible, our own arms encircle us and we contain our pain.

Does life, or God, what is the difference, build us with accepted experience, stab by stab of accepted understanding? As though each joy or sorrow is God, or life, saying, "You see?" and we are needed, not forced, to say truly, "I see". It is like anaesthetic revelations in *Varieties of Religious Experience* when the inadequately drugged patient felt the knife, and at each cut she saw God enabled to make a bend in the path on which He walked. When we know He can.

Is it possible that the old can stand any loss better than their intense relationship with themselves? If we are free from pain and disharmony, though idle, uncomfortable and alone, is awareness enough? But for how long, and how much alone? Without loving letters, and with no friendly voice on the 'phone, lacking the loyal concern of one's family? May I never have that to face, but still— the basic need for me is to meet alone and in silence all that puzzles and pains me and to wait until the turmoil is stilled.

Hardihood is a quality supposedly created by difficulty, and I have always felt it to be a stimulating virtue. I like people who have it, and that must mean that I like people who have been disciplined by hardship, which is true. I find them realistic, not easily daunted, and they make few childish claims. This also means that the hardness of life I deplore creates the qualities I admire. Poverty used to seem to create morality. If you were poor you had to be selfless, uncomplaining, independent, ingenious, and courageous. Now in an age of plenty when it is felt that we should have what we want—and when this becomes a practical possibility—what happens to hardihood? Is it a disappearing virtue? I should be sorry to see it go, and very surprised if it did.

We are told that the over-indulged child having had little hardship lacks hardihood, and the weak boy has to be violent to respect himself, so hardihood is wanted and missed. Children must still have to endure the natural rage of parents, and there is no doubt at all that parents have to summon a wealth of hardihood to endure their children. Even plenty requires a good deal of fortitude. To organise family transport with only two cars, to find leisure or quiet in a house equipped with every machine a modern house can contain is not easy. To combine chores with responsible jobs, not to mention illness, accidents, and the new poverty of the highly paid, all this demands stamina of the highest order, for the strain of it is great. Now when so many have so much, many work harder than their forbears. So why does having much create strain, dissatisfaction and confusion? Could it be that austerity kept life simple, simple pleasures remaining real pleasures, while plenty makes for complication, and having much leaves us sated?

The power to differentiate used to be taken as the sign of a fine mind, marking the road to wisdom. Is the present longing not to have differences noted a just claim that common humanity is more

important than individual quality, that our re-
semblances are more numerous than our differences? This is the problem that confronts us, and
what is the answer? Modernity demands inclusion of the weakest side, the lowest point, indi-
vidually and socially. Nothing must be excluded,
so where are we? Can strength encompass weakness, or will weakness undermine strength? Is
our civilization falling or rising? Must we face
the possibility of another dark age, sheltering the
great values in our hearts until they are once
more prized, or can we open to unheard of good?
No answer is possible. No new pattern of living
is yet clear.

Looking out on the world I am no longer in,
it feels as though we will to be undifferentiated.
This must have meaning though the meaning is
still hidden from us. It could be a justified recoil,
loss of heart, lack of courage, remembering the
last sixty years. Yet think what mankind has
borne, who could plumb the valour that lies in
the human heart? We must wait and hope and
watch. Take note of every reflection of the gen-

eral situation that arises in our own hearts. Assess, wait—open and aware.

If differentiation has seemed part basis of morality, clarity and order, no wonder the present demand to be accepted without assessment sounds like a demand not to be judged at all. This could be a lowering of life, a recession to the inchoate, and a relinquishment of the responsibility of the individual.

"Judge not that ye be not judged" and "Love your neighbour as yourself" make me wonder and question. Not to judge can be the result of humility and compassion, but even then we must remain clear as to what it is from which we withhold judgement. If we do not condemn is it because we know we are not fit to do so, or is it that the necessity of value in men has become a concept of little interest? New values will not be defined in the time of the old, so we are uncertain, our minds tired by doubt.

The Measure of My Days

And our neighbour—our neighbour who is crowding us very close these days—what of him, who is he? I have never been sure whether he was the kind people who are near and trusted, and of course the railway porter who can on occasion be a ministering angel, and naturally all the people in the shops, for if you live in a small town and are really old you wonder who is not your neighbour. But is my neighbour the lout I observe, or the author I read when I am advised to "keep up with the times"—he who expresses spleen for spleen's sake—for these I cannot love. Is the plain fact then that our neighbour is often not easy to love, and most of the time we do not love him? What is more, out of honesty to him, and to oneself, we judge both him and ourselves, we must, in order to know our dislikes and his, or how else is there any reality? If we do not recognise our instinctive recoil (and sometimes it is the wise animal in us giving warning), how are we to have the courage to take our stand? If we are judged, if we do not feel the recoil from us, then what is there to make us pause and judge ourselves?

The cry for an egalitarian society is so strong that it may be the new and needed truth, but the opposing truth flames in my heart, and difference, the precious difference of the individual, sharpens in my thoughts. The difference that is innate in nature—nature whose law is diversity —the difference that is also our most difficult achievement and chief honour must have full recognition or else equality becomes uniformity. It is the individual who can stand alone that can best relate to another person, it is he who can be true to a bond, and it is he who possesses a creative mind. Anyone who has become himself will respect himself for his difference and so be respected by all. But this is not equality. Only identical things are equal, and nature is incapable of repeating herself, great artist that she is, so what is the cry for equality, and what will it bring?

We are different, not equal, so we suffer and compete, rise and fall, lose and achieve ourselves.

We are truly the vehicles of evolution because under stress we make a decisive choice that creates change, enforced by necessity. Necessity can be cruel, and any generous heart and just mind tries to control the inequalities of circumstance. Great good can come from greater equality, less suffering, a flowering of new talent, new pride, increase in understanding, but there is also a danger now seen and weighed. It is the decrease of individuality on a large scale.

Unreal inequality can stimulate to action, but unreal equality seems to dissolve us and distort us. We tend to live at the collective level, undefined, unreal because of claims in our natures that we have not fulfilled, because of differences we have evaded. This is recognised as a present danger, and the word "depersonalized" is used to describe it.

Thoughtful writers in America dwell on the degree of emptiness reached there, middle-aged couples are frightened children, afraid to be alone, only able to live by melting into their Club, their neighbours. English analysts are burdened and baffled by what they call the non-ego patient, people who are not pathological, but who lack the ability to live their own lives, needing to be carried. It is understandable to assume that fewer differences would mean less suffering, but it is dangerous to create large numbers of people whose first claim is to avoid the inner struggle, the ordeal of self-discovery.

Modern permissiveness makes it difficult to tell good from bad, as though it were simpler to have no differences at all. We used to dislike and condemn our own faults when we saw them in others, so that we parked out our sins on our neighbours where they at least existed for us. Now that it is uncertain when a fault is a fault our vagueness increases. Add to evasion and uncertainty the fact that we tend to annul the heights and depths of experience. If we no longer seek the spirit, if love and relationship should become small because sexual experience has few barriers around it to mark it as important, if the sense of sin is no longer self-recognition, then where is the intensity of our humanity?

Equality could become our greatest danger as

it becomes more true of greater numbers, who live not from the depths built in the past, nor from the uniqueness knit from self-knowledge, but at the herd level where the human being tends to be depotentialised. Facing this with the gravity it warrants may be the truest way to lessen dangers more feared.

These suppositions seem true to me, but I also believe that there is an increase in honesty, in insight, of which some are aware and thus are able to live a larger area of their natures, so that there is an increase in individuality. In fact, we have a new inequality.

I am so caught in my own experience of age that it occurs to me only now that it matters who speaks of age, and anyone would have the right to ask, "By what road did you arrive where you are? What experiences formed your viewpoint?". For over twenty-five years I was a Jungian analyst, and it is this experience, those long years of observation that force on me the idea that modernity is like an analysis in reverse. Instead of gathering oneself together, it is a dispersal of oneself.

In analysis, as I have known it, you are confronted by your qualities and cannot disown them, though you try to. The animal, the primitive, the child, the crowd, the hero, the criminal, both sexes, the initiate, they are all in you. They appear in your dreams, you cannot deny them. By becoming responsible for them, in as far as you do, you know the pain of becoming conscious. This is made endurable and creative by figures beyond the personal, wisdom greater than yours, mysteries inspiring awe, all formed, one has to presume, by the endless generations whom life has presented with the same problems we all share. This rich and searing process of gathering a centre where you know what you are and are not makes me feel at moments as though modern ethics are a vast evasion. Of what? Subjective values, cause and effect, a many-sided reality that I miss and cannot name.

The Measure of My Days

It is easier to be everyone rather than integrate diversity in yourself, but is the ease not paid for in human quality? In analysis, while never forgetting the degree of one's own incurability, one experiences eternal truths that give dignity to man. Is that a frequent experience today?

If in this time of planning for order there seems to be an increase of disorder, is it not possible by the strange swing of the opposites that the young as they mature will make a new choice, having tried many ways, and create an order we do not yet see? Will necessity, which can be as good a taskmaster as analysis, teach us that we are contained in an order we do not understand. And how many will accept the discipline of the discovery?

To be dominated by abstract ideas is part of the helplessness of age. Is my emptiness invaded, or do I try to come nearer to my kind by viewing their problems from my isolation? I care, I am torn with care for the quality of humanity. If I suffer fruitlessly, guttering candle that I am, I choose to burn to the end. Though it is mostly under protest. That is understood.

While equality is thought possible, even a basic right, I want to remember the stimulus and interest of inequality. At once I feel heartless, as though I might wound or dishonour someone who had had less than I. The degree of our lack naturally determines the keenness of our claim. I have lacked much, vital things, and the ache has spurred me to intense living. But isn't reality the rousing shock we all need, and do we not lose ourselves in pretence if the truth and tragedy of inequality is not accepted? If we could be equal,

The Measure of My Days

what would happen to reverence and compassion?

When I see nature's inherent inequality, I melt and want to be tender. If one is going to be truthful one has to be very tender. To respect difference, to try to understand difference is the only way. The imagination must be stretched to its widest, every wince of self-knowledge accepted, all this of course, but never accept the utter unreality of wishing for equality. It would mean that individuality went, goals vanished, and you sank in the static. I cannot see it as a fact, but hear it as the cry of unlived pride.

Who would be equal to whom? Do we all go as low as we can to prove we are above no one? Must all the gifts of those greater than we disappear from the world? No triumphs of accomplishment? No drive to discover the rare in ourselves and others? Never to be bemused by beauties we lack? No sudden insight of what might be? No respect or loyalty or humility stirred by what you had not known was possible? But these are our ennobling moments. It is at these times we outgrow ourselves.

Inequality entails resentment, envy, hate, galling realizations, all bitter lessons teaching us who we are as nothing else can; but also teaching us the drama and hope of life's chaos. New knowledge brings sharp pain, and it can come to the very young. Shyness, self-consciousness can etch your pattern in you like an acid. A hot blush at a blunder is the birth pain of perception, and when you see ease and restraint and simple statement all in one you enter your right world.

No superiors? But nothing is as precious to me as my superiors. I cannot let them go, the milestones of my life. From my earliest days shyness held me, hesitation increased as I took in the variety of good I could neither have nor be. Yet it is just here that imagination stirs and world on world appears for exploration.

Admiration is one of the chief delights of living. Interest, increasing to ardour, finding others who agree, one igniting another, and when it is certain that there is far, far too much to be taken in one reaches the bliss of being carefree. You cherish the friends and impressions that have

The Measure of My Days

proved to belong to you and let all the rest go. You have reached a place where you are humble, where you are in fact your own size, and you rest in a contentment between that of the child and the sage; the former not having begun to notice difference, the latter beyond stressing it.

All through history there have been periods dominated by an idea too highly charged with passion, too hot to touch with safety; race is such a subject now. It voices the longing for equality, which also fired the woman's movement, and equality is so stressed that I wonder if the need for identity does not lie behind it. The overriding problem of this age is perhaps the need to create identity and the recoil from the demands of the task. It may be that a struggle is going on in most of us between the desire to create our own difference and the longing to gain ease and power by joining the mass. What travail to strike a balance here. Perhaps the creating of identity is man's most essential task, and if we demand to be given it as a right, we have not even guessed that it is our life's work to create it.

Equality has only existed in the simplest forms of society, yet now the wish for it is so strong that it creates everything from strikes to wars. Has the complexity of life increased until it is hardly bearable? Frog spawn seeming the last stage that was at all comfortable. There is an element of despair in this age, for many inequalities are inherent in nature and cannot be changed.

The desire for equality is making people live by imitation. Is it good for the men of many nations, and the women as well, to attempt to copy the white man? They seem to model themselves on what he has slowly, blindly and not blindly, painfully and shamefully, and splendidly made himself. Western man is almost the world prototype, and the more people who distort themselves to resemble him and so be his equal, the more he could be hated. He may be envied for his achievements, power and possessions, but he could also be hated by those who have falsified themselves to gain what he has, and because they hope some day to punish him for his conviction of his own superiority. He has mastered matter, and he has outlined himself. His outline is very clear.

Many races, and most women, have remained nearer to their instincts and traditions, and they can seem undefined. This may be part cause of the unease and enmity that stirs. Western man has been so sure, so in command, that he does not guess what impression he makes on those who have developed differently. He has so seldom been regarded as inferior, and almost never as invisible—a not uncommon experience for others—that there is a blindness in him that could be counted a weakness.

If it is greater self-definition that lies before women, and greater concrete achievement that lies before the less organised races, much may be gained, but easy definition has its own sterility, while the undefined can be the very quick of life. Many will always live it, remaining close to their source for the increase of life they gain. It will be at our peril if we put all our faith in the measurable, and dishonour that which lies beyond statement.

Perhaps the less differentiated people are still natural enough to evolve a good that we lost a long way back, so Western races almost owe other races a warning. We might say, "We are bad guides for you to follow. Our way could be your undoing. We have become factual, mechanical, theoretical and over active. We try to be as efficient, untiring and reliable as machines. This cannot be a good time for Western man to be imitated as he is too near a recoil from himself." And small wonder our sense of awe has almost gone, little is sacred to us, we have lost the grace of innate well-being, and how often can we admire and revere? "Follow your own way," we should say, "but don't follow us".

65

The Measure of My Days

I often want to say to people, "You have neat, tight expectations of what life ought to give you, but you won't get it. That isn't what life does. Life does not accommodate you, it shatters you. It is meant to, and it couldn't do it better. Every seed destroys its container or else there would be no fruition."

But some wouldn't hear, and some would shatter themselves on principle.

A note book might be the very thing for all the old who wave away crossword puzzles, painting, petit point, and knitting. It is more restful than conversation, and for me it has become a companion, more a confessional. It cannot shrive me, but knowing myself better comes near to that. Only this morning—this mild, sunny morning that charmed me into happiness—I realized my cheer was partly because I was alone. I thought for an awful moment that perhaps I was essentially unloving, perhaps had never loved; but years of absorption, and of joy, yes, I have loved, but enough? Is there any stab as deep as wondering where and how much you failed those you loved? Disliking is my great sin, which I cannot overcome. It has taken me my entire life to learn not to withdraw.

I wonder why love is so often equated with joy when it is everything else as well. Devastation, balm, obsession, granting and receiving excessive value, and losing it again. It is recognition, often of what you are not but might be. It sears and it heals. It is beyond pity and above law. It can seem like truth. But what is truth? Oh this mysterious world in which we know nothing, nothing. At times love seems clarity, beyond judgement. But this is a place that can also be reached alone, an impersonal place, found and lost again.

Love is asked to carry intolerable burdens, not

seen from outside. Love can be hard service, giving your all, and it may be finding your all. It is
sometimes a discipline enabling you to do the impossible. It may be your glimpse of transcen-
dence. It is even agreement. But it is all the
pains as well, the small pains as well as the great.
It is baffling to be loved by someone incapable of
seeing you. It is pain to have your love claimed
as a cloak that another may hide from himself.
Love tested by its indulgence to weakness, or its
blindness to unworthiness can turn to scorn. Love
may have blind facets in its all-seeing eyes, but
it is we who are blind to what we ask it to bear.
Of course it is the heights and the depths, the
follies and the glories, but being loving is not
always love, and hate can be more cleansing.
Why are love and hate near each other, opposite,
and alike, and quickly interchangeable?

Love is honoured and hate condemned, but love
can do harm. It can soften, distort, maintain the

unreal, and cover hate. Hate can be nature's way of forcing honesty on us, and finding the strength to follow a truer way. But as hate is a burning poison that dehumanises us, how can I be anything but appalled by it? I am appalled. I have hated, and I know its evil. But hate is part of truth. It is not safe to forget that the Orphic World Egg had on one side the face of Eros, and on the other that of Phobus, and no one who has seen either ever forgets.

When I was young I knew inside me what I could and could not accept, but I could not express opposition. I had to bear the unacceptable a long time until I hated it. Then I could protest, but with the scalding accompaniment of hate. I know well that hate is a consuming fire poisoning every part of us, yet—yet there are times when it has to be met, for some degree of it is as cleansing as fire. Heat brings change, and so anger can be the right weapon if one is clean enough to use it.

Apparently hate and definition belong together. What differs from you, you may hate;

perhaps too quickly, perhaps too slowly. It may be from fear, fear for your identity, fear of your inability to guard your weak identity. Could it be that at our archaic level we are so undifferentiated, so in a state of primal oneness that anything different feels a threat, and hate flames to protect us, is needed, as our dissolution is very possible. So the deep point in us is a dark, hot oneness, making difference a thing to dread and combat. Differing is never a cool thing, and it is the differing, not the issue that makes human beings boil, so no wonder believing what the crowd believes is a comfort and a power. Yet love, too, is a oneness, a warmth and a power, but utterly different, since it is personal, willing to face difference, and even capable of relinquishing its need.

Before the First World War I was travelling in France and when the train stopped a middle-aged woman entered the compartment accompanied by a distraught-looking girl of perhaps seventeen who held a handkerchief to her eyes. The woman announced quietly but gravely and dramatically, *"C'est l'amour"*. At once the five or six other passengers rearranged themselves, leaving one side of the compartment vacant. The young girl laid herself down at full length, her head in her mother's lap, a cloak over her, and softly sobbed herself to sleep. The other passengers sat crowded in silent respect. A god had struck, and it was best to be wary.

Differing and belonging is only one of our problems, but so important that without those two strong threads binding each other there would be no living cloth, usable and durable. How much containment is necessary, of how much daring and originality are we capable? Man's pugnacity and his evasions must be made up of this question. We, our pattern, what makes us ourselves to ourselves, can be destroyed by alien influences, yet without the new we may be stultified. It takes great courage to open our minds and hearts, yet it is required of us to our last breath.

I don't always moan over humanity. I marvel at the artistry and toughness there often is in small hidden tribes, isolated peoples, small nations who put all their energy into creating their own patterns. What but being different brings the conviction of having found the best way? With endurance revered, rewards certain, behaviour settled, then energy flows in patterns of satisfaction. The satisfaction of creating your unique way could account for every totem, custom, and superstition; with all doubt gone as to right and wrong, each member knowing his place in the group, and knowing his group to be like no other, what more was needed to survive? Only placating the forces of nature, in reality as well as in symbol. The pattern that necessity had formed made each individual live creatively to keep it in being. This makes the highly stylized group the prototype of the individual, so only where the group is comparatively small is the individual and the group at one.

Any small tribe spending their energies in their pattern of yearly renewal would seem to be more satisfied than modern man, no matter what their material difficulties, or just because of their material difficulties. They are fully occupied in the vital elaboration of their own identity, as well as their survival. This is their safety and their religion. This is the precious secret their wise men harbour. From this comes their self-decoration, their art, their culture.

An intense sense of their own identity may entail avoidance of other groups, also fear and hostility. If they should mix or intermarry, uncertainty could follow, blurring of beliefs, doubt, and perhaps despair. It could be suicidal not to hate the alien way. If this is at all true must we say that our present belief in oneness, integration, organisation which we follow blindly, could result in the individual becoming nobody, nothing? Are numbers our true enemy, our undoing

. . . if I could stop worrying about what is beyond me.

But I can't. Was sameness inevitable from the time of easy communication; going to places that differ from ours making them differ less, a too easy exchange of goods making them less worthy of exchange? Then do comfort, safety, order, fraternity, all the values that our intelligence and compassion create, endanger us? Is it the terrible truth that our abilities, our open minds, and generous hearts are self-destructive? Do we have to assume that man is incapable of knowing what is for his own good? Is he to be forever blind to the fact that it is his own quality of being that alone matters? Man can do almost everything but assess himself. "Know thyself" is still the unbearable command. But it is tried. Oh it is tried.

Then I should know that good is sure to bring some bad, as bad some good. The bad that results from the good done brings the next problem in the great chain of life, each requiring deeper understanding. It does take the heart of a hero to even glance at what one hopes is the wavering line of growth.

It is puzzling that many seem relieved to have got rid of God; no sense of impoverishment at all. It is almost as though they had been personally irked by that unknowable, inescapable power. Some even seem a little vain and preen themselves, as though it had been partly they who had destroyed their creator, and that of the world as well. They feel no loss, apparently. They are not surprised that the world still exists.

To destroy a god used to require a hero, one who was fit to be a god, and dared assume the burden. Now it takes no hero. Secularity is voiced with relief until one wonders—will poverty again be the birthplace of a new-born god? An inner poverty this time. Love is said to be the child of need, and that we have, and will have more.

My *only fear about death* is that it will not come soon enough. Life still interests and occupies me. Happily I am not in such discomfort that I wish for death, I love and am loved, but please God I die before I lose my independence. I do not know what I believe about life after death; if it exists then I burn with interest, if not—well, I am tired. I have endured the flame of living and that should be enough. I have made others suffer, and if there are more lives to be lived I believe I ought to do penance for the suffering I have caused. I should experience what I have made others experience. It belongs to me, and I should learn it.

If I suffer from my lacks, and I do daily, I also feel elation at what I have become. At times I feel a sort of intoxication because of some small degree of gain; as though the life that is in me has been my charge, the trust birth brought me, and my blunders, sins, the blanks in me as well as the gifts, have in some long painful transmutation made the life that is in me clearer.

The most important thing in my life was the

rich experience of the unconscious. This was a gift life gave me and I only had the sense to honour and serve it. It taught me that we are fed by great forces, and I know that I am in the hands of what seemed immortal. It hardly matters whether I am mortal or not since I have experienced the immortal. This makes me at rest in much of my being, but not in all. It is almost as if the order in me is barely me, and I still have to deal with the chaos that is mine.

It has taken me all the time I've had to become myself, yet now that I am old there are times when I feel I am barely here, no room for me at all. I remember that in the last months of my pregnancies the child seemed to claim almost all my body, my strength, my breath, and I held on wondering if my burden was my enemy, uncertain as to whether my life was at all mine. Is life a pregnancy? That would make death a birth.

The Measure of My Days

When I recall those nights when I tried to understand, letting the thrust of truth teach me a deeper truth, how sexual that was. This has never occurred to me before. Then understanding can resemble impregnation. My understanding was not thought, so I wonder what it was. Could it have been feminine thought, right for us, not dry and arid as man's thought so often is when it is used by women; or could it have been assessing by true feeling? It was a highly disciplined acceptance of the value of truth, no evasion allowed, so it may have been a feeling judgement.

The enchantment of the sky, ever changing beauty almost ignored. Beyond words, without fixed form, not to be understood, or stated. It ravishes away dullness, worry, even pain. It graces life when nothing else does. It is the first marvel of the day. Even when leaden grey it is still a friend, withdrawn for a time.

Evolution is necessarily slow since we resent it so. A large proportion of our energy is used in holding it back, wanting to stop it if possible. The new good is refused countless times before it is accepted. The rare, the beautiful, the admirable are taken as rebukes, making us feel inferior, suggesting our improvement. Anything but that, so we mock at the new, recoil from the rare, belittle the great, until finally grown accustomed . . . to ignore is easy.

I am ashamed to admit to myself that I am disappointed in humanity. Nothing less. That is the ache that lies behind other aches. Not disappointed in this beautiful world, owing much of its beauty to man, but somehow broken-hearted at the incorrigibility of man. The animals know how to live and be beautiful and themselves; primitive peoples evolve religions that give meaning to their lives. But as soon as consciousness arrives man begins his blunders. His genius is for creating insoluble problems, every cure creating new difficulties. How could it be otherwise since consciousness is the intolerable registering of pain and pleasure, opinion and belief. Consciousness seems to be both what life strives to evolve and its greatest danger.

Mercy seems an undoubted good, yet it can bring ill results. Everyone wants it as I would want it; one side of me would plead for mercy for all my blind acts, for all I haven't been. I think, I cannot be sure, but I think I would rather be cleansed than granted mercy. No, no, I am quite sure, I want both, and because I need mercy I pray that I may feel it for others, that I may make life a little less hard, still seeing clearly that we have to give pain, cannot avoid it, that we are unceasingly burdens one to another. We are indeed each beholden to each. Oh love is truly the child of need, but realism, just realism, admitting what we are and what we do, is the smiting of the rock that makes tenderness and pity flow.

I have to go on with my thoughts, knowing they are not thoughts, but more like sobs or counter-blows, perhaps just worries of an old heart. I could not see more clearly than I do that impersonal judgements are beyond me, beyond all but the very wise, the well-informed who relinquish judgement and observe. Yet if some kindly priest remonstrated with me saying, "These are not matters for your concern", I would say—"If my heart aches for humanity, let it be so"

It feels right to take humanity into my heart, or out of my heart and examine it and be eased of it. Poor, poor mankind what a marvel it is, what marvels man has done. His buildings alone would make one assume him an archangel. His music, his order, the richness of his acts—it is because of marvels accomplished that we have high hopes—and when man refuses much of the time to live up to the range of the mighty creature he sometimes is, then hopeful people like me make a to-do. When we see what mankind can do, and be—and we have no idea why it is so

The Measure of My Days

much easier to do than to be—and when with
equal clarity we see what he usually is, then
childishly, shamefully we cry, "Won't more people be strong, and wise and lovable, because I
try and I can't". Yet even in my despair I see
man rise to such noble heights in his fateful
struggle, that more often than we guess the
gods may regard him with brotherly awe.

Of course one is forced to deplore and revere humanity. Its variety, disparity, and complexity
make it the great cross on which we are
stretched. We are crucified in experiencing ourselves. The cross is our cross because it is we
who are the nobilities and beauties and delicious
happiness, and the horrors and the indifference
and the blindness. How could we react to suffering and joy with anything but the full range of
our possibilities? With my thoughts stabbing
like spears it might be supposed that I have
waited for my eighty-third year before I noticed

mankind. This is not so. I never found it possible to ignore man's plight even when I was busy living it, and now in my idleness it has me by the scruff of the neck. I have to endure it as though there was a final bite that would yield a last drop of understanding blood. Can this be true? What must I see?

One thing I see clearly. These notes are not thoughts. They are the creaks and cries of a heart opening slowly. So love has nothing to do with liking. I see. Concern lay in the depths when on the surface I felt recoil. I do see.

Do we then begin to see that all evil is ours? Not belittling evil in the hopes of remaining little ourselves. Do we prepare for a wholeness never yet attempted with open eyes; wholeness large enough to contain what—who dares define how much?

Are we about to say—at least within centuries

of saying—"With the help of the God within me I accept responsibility for my own acts—all, all, especially for those I did not know were mine"? If that great task is beginning, then we live in an age of promise, and who would not be reckless enough to hope?

There is youth in me, in most of us, who would be carefree and happy, "bird happy", and would find it natural and enough. Knowing that destruction and creation are twin brothers, that the gods destroy and create—why else are they called gods?—I hear without surprise someone in me saying: "But life is delicious, what beauty, what interest, I wouldn't have missed it for worlds. Look at the day, feel the air, you see for yourself, all is well."

Christ gave love as the sole solution for man's justified hatred of man, and we try, and we have improved, but we don't make it work. Christ asked us to choose God, not life, and now many choose life without God. If God is the central meaning of life, and it feels so, we do not know how to live that way. We have tried so many ways and have let them become bigotry, or tyranny, or dreary pretence. We crave for that which lies behind the terrible play of the opposites. We pray to have the conflict resolved, but life would end if it were resolved. To endure it must be our creative role, nothing else seems true. If it is only at the centre of our being that suffering is resolved, is it not there that we are nearest to God? Is it even the road to him if we knew how to travel it?

My presumption in thinking badly of life mortifies me. What do I know? How dare I judge? I don't. I feel shame, and yet—life is cruel; and exquisitively kind. Put the sound of softly lapping waves and a clear green sky in the scales, and how many woes would it take to strike a balance? If I regret none of the bad things that have happened to me, knowing that I needed them all to reach any ripeness, then is all hardship justified if someone learns by it? No, there is much too much. So I do judge? Yes, every second of the day. I say to life: "You are very hard", and I also say: "We are blind, we prefer to be blind. It is easier. We are mean and small, we choose to be small. It has a bite to it". Life has to be hard to have any effect on us; even now we hardly notice it. Beyond that can one go? I must. I add, "We are also blind to the miracles of good that come to us. We hardly heed them, we even protest against them". Then I am left where I was, appalled by the hardness of life, knowing we are forced to be unwilling heroes. Suddenly I wonder—is all hardness justified because we are so slow in realizing that life was meant to be heroic? Greatness is required of us. That is life's aim and justification, and we poor fools have for centuries been trying to make it convenient, manageable, pliant to our will. It is also peaceful and tender and funny and dull. Yes, all that.

Good things have gone, some good things will always go when new things come, and we mourn. We may mourn rightly, for the outlook is uncertain, perhaps very dark. Destruction is part of creativity, that is the terrible truth we shrink from, knowing it may be misused. This truth is everywhere, almost too obvious to be felt. It is leaden in the old who are being destroyed by time, and I admit that it takes more courage than I had known to drink the lees of life.

My note book shows me how much I mourn. Perhaps the forms of life that are passing should be mourned, and this may be the right role of age. Perhaps our wail should be part of the paean of life that is being lived. I do not mourn for lost happiness, I do not mourn for myself. I mourn that life is so incomprehensible, and I mourn for this confused age. We old are the wailers. I hear us everywhere.

The Measure of My Days

Within the last month I have had two odd en-
counters. After waiting for some moments while
heavy traffic passed I crossed the road with a
comely woman of seventy or so. As we arrived
safely on the other side she bowed and said, "It
was such a beautiful world they destroyed". I
bowed and we parted. Then a week later, waiting
in a small railway station, I heard a woman with
clear, brave eyes, well over sixty, saying that
she had lived for the past thirty years on the edge
of a desert, and she commented to all of us, "I
think you lead a dreadful life here". The woman
next to her spoke and gave what was almost a
cry, "Life could be glorious if we would let it
be". I felt she was perhaps a little mad, but what
made her so?

I wonder if old people want truth more than anything else, and they cannot find it. Perhaps truth
is diversity so each seeks his own. Is truth a
thing in itself, a state of consciousness to which
we are opaque or clear?

I admire a contented mind. I revere enjoyment of simple things. I can imagine that contentment has a high degree of truth. But the human tendency is to take good as normal, and one's natural right, and so no cause for satisfaction or pleasure. This is accompanied by the habit of regarding bad as abnormal and a personal outrage.

The woman who has a gift for old age is the woman who delights in comfort. If warmth is known as the blessing it is, if your bed, your bath, your best-liked food and drink are regarded as fresh delights, then you know how to thrive when old. If you get the things you like on the simplest possible terms, serve yourself lightly, efficiently and calmly, all is almost well. If you are truly calm you stand a chance of surviving much, but calmness is intermittent with me. Sensuous pleasure seems necessary to old age as intellectual pleasure palls a little. At times music justifies living, but mere volume of sound can overwhelm, and I find silence exquisite. I have spent my whole life reading, only to find that most of it is lost, so books no longer have their former command. I live by rectitude or reverence, or courtesy, by being ready in case life calls, all lightly peppered with despair. This makes me rest on comfort. I could use the beauty and dignity of a cat but, denied that, I try for her quiet.

April 3rd

I am home, I am home, I am home. I have been home for a week so that it is now natural to be here, but my joy is more than natural. I have life before me, better health, and less pain, less pain; the biggest pain gone for good, only bits of chronic pain left, sharp discomfort say, left to bother me. Not to have pain, even my degree of pain, which was always bearable, is a constant elation which will always be part of me.

When the surgeon looked at me with honest

eyes and said I must have an operation, that my age was not against it, that I could not be out of pain with so bad a gall bladder, and that without it I had every chance of normal health, everything became simple and settled. I was given medicine that dulled the pain while I waited for a room in the Nursing Home. My spirits danced. I was gay, gay that I was to lose pain. Everyone was full of concern but I laughed inside. All that time when I had been in pain, when I was a burden to myself, a problem to doctors, and unconvincing to my family and friends, was over. I basked in the respect paid to an operation. People said I was brave. I wasn't brave, I was happy.

Of course I might die, I had heard of the heart giving out under an operation, it was possible, but then I would meet the great mystery. It almost seemed my chance. A mean way of slipping out though, not fair to the surgeon, and I want to be conscious that I am dying. I did not want to die, but I have lived my life—or so I used to feel. Now each extra day is a gift. An

extra day in which I may gain some new understanding, see a beauty, feel love, or know the
richness of watching my youngest grandson
express his every like and dislike with force and
sweetness. But all this is the sentience by which
I survive, and who knows, it may matter deeply
how we end so mysterious a thing as living.

I had one fear. What if something went wrong,
and I became an invalid? What if I became a
burden, ceased to be a person and became a
problem, a patient, someone who could not die?
That was my one fear, but my chances were
reasonably good, so all was simple and settled
and out of my hands. Being ill in a nursing home
became my next task, a sombre dance in which
I knew some of the steps. I must conform. I must
be correct. I must be meek, obedient and grateful,
on no account must I be surprising. If I de-
viated by the breadth of a toothbrush I would be
in the wrong.

The Measure of My Days

A book of poems I had ordered weeks before arrived as I left for the Nursing Home, and they occupied me during that long evening when I lay waiting for time to pass. Finally the night began when my body belonged to brisk strangers. The ugliness of my age was exposed to trim, fresh women. I was at last sent to have a bath at five in the morning, and then more drugs, and the strangeness of knowing less and less until knowing ceased.

Next day I was told that all was over and all had gone well. I was lost in pain and drugs and that was the only truly bad day. I thought I was screaming with pain, I could feel the screams in my throat, but days later I asked Sister and she said I had not made a sound, that few did. So it was part of the fog I was in. By the third day a sense of achievement came for I was doing my task well, no mistakes so far, and already there was that sense that came six years before when I had a fractured femur. Then I had felt so frail and weary of life that it seemed as though I had met defeat. To learn to walk again seemed beyond me. Then strength arrived and forced me to recognize that just because this accident had happened I was stronger. Where the strength and the will to use it had come from I could not imagine, but who understands the ebb and flow of energy? At first I did not believe in this new strength, but it was there, vital, mine. Now after the operation some new life was near. I must use it carefully, rest on it, test it. There was not enough yet to feel anything but hope, yet it was in the offing, I recognised it, I must do my work of being a patient with care. This was work that one did by lying still, remembering, judging. Deciding when your discomfort justified asking for help, and when it was the youness of you. I made some mistakes and then I was contrite and very reasonable. Patients must like and dislike as little as possible.

On the fourth, or was it the fifth day I saw the great wound healed for most of its length. If my body could do that then surely I could do all my body wanted of me. Then I began to feel so well that I knew I was in danger of breaking rules.

I must not. I must remember that this new vitality was partly the strength that comes to me when needed, and partly sheer exhilaration, always my undoing. I must be quiet. I would woo each nurse so that rules would slacken a little, and then I would know them as woman to woman. The goodness of most of the nurses was real; some radiated goodness, one had beauty, two used professional virtue to cover bitterness, but bit by bit we blent civility with humanity and liked each other.

Then the rage I knew so well rose in me and threatened all. I heard the animal growl in me when they did all the things it is my precious privacy and independence to do for myself. I hated them while I breathed, "Thank you, nurse". At last I was allowed a bath in a tub, though with a nurse to direct my every move, and in a burst of naturalness I told her that being ill made me bad tempered, and while they were being kind and caring for me I wanted to say, "Let me alone, I'll do it myself", and oh my relief when the dear woman laughed and said,

"You're the kind that get well quickly. Some want everything done for them, just won't take themselves on at all".

More and more I belonged to myself. I hopped from my bed and watered my flowers, careful not to leave a petal where it should not be. On perhaps the seventh or eighth morning I could see that the sun was shining, even the black silk bandage I wore over my eyes showed that, and before anyone had come in, at what seemed an early hour—though I had accepted that time in a Nursing Home was different from other time—I got up, threw back the curtains, opened all four windows—they would not open very wide—and expanded into the blue sky. Or so my whole heart longed to do. I wanted to be out of my body, without limit, I was rejuvenated, young, I wanted a future. I was still eighty-two, they had done nothing about that, and I wanted to scale the sky.

I remembered that yesterday four aircraft had flown in repeating circles, crossing and recrossing, and I knew that would satisfy me.

A moment more of joy, and I drew the curtains, resumed my black bandage, and sleepily greeted nurse when she entered with the crisp cheer of someone who has been on night duty. Later I noticed the little window in the door through which nurses assure themselves that all is well.

I was strong enough on the twelfth day to go to a non-surgical Nursing Home, and there I could look at the sea, the coast, the cliffs, and take two short walks a day. I felt so well that I thought it was the air that was curing me, for now I did everything for myself, even making my bed. Then it seemed the quiet of the scene that steadied me—the cliffs, the sea; I spent hours with a book in my hand but watching gulls and clouds. I was told that the immutable land was always moving, sliding, falling, even the caves rich in fossils almost lost now; so the land was movement, the water was movement, and the wind, mist, sunshine, rain were change, nothing was still.

I took a day or two to realize that most of the patients were too old to leave their rooms. One still strong enough to tidy her room daily was a hundred and two. She longed to die, had given up eating as the one permissible way, but became so hungry that she had to begin eating again. I was among people who could not die. How many longed to? Who should? Who can say? We cannot know what dying is. Is there a right moment for each of us? If we have hardly lived at all, it may be much harder to die. We may have to learn that we failed to live our lives. Looking at the old from outside I think—"Let them go, there is no one there. They have already gone, and left their bodies behind. Make a law that is impossible to abuse, and allow release". But inside the old, who makes the final decision? They are mysteries like everything else.

The nursing was good, homely and warm, natural compassion from country girls and kindly women. One sister was simple virtue, complete as a pearl. I asked, I had to know, was nursing the old depressing; could nurses do it only for short periods as no cure was possible? They seemed surprised and said that old people were dears, and needed help so much that everyone liked nursing them. I had seen with what grace and gentleness the nurses behaved, so here was a good that life would be poorer without, and my rational reaction was an ugly thing beside it.

Good Friday

I do not know why the day on which man denied God should be called good. If Christ, who was both man and God, had to experience man's refusal of the spirit, man still seems undisturbed by what he did and does. Christ as man knew God. His very being said, "I am man and God, and so it is with each of you". We struggle to hear that, and understand it and live it, but it slips from us as though it hardly mattered, also as though it can be taken for granted. We do not know what we mean by "God" or "Man" or

"Life" and the drama of its contradiction and resolution is everything. It is also the actual, terrible inclusion of evil, for good would have no meaning without evil, and if man had not crucified Christ, saying by his act, "We do not want the spirit, relieve us of it, we choose our blindness", we would have lacked this lesson in what evil man can do. We cannot seem to learn evil by living its depths again and again, so how can we learn good? What a blessing that much of the time we live both with no thought of either.

I am rereading after fifty years Henry Adams's *Mont-St.-Michel.* One of the pleasures of age is reading books long forgotten, with only the enlargement they once brought remembered. As Henry Adams tells of that great flowering of trust in the Virgin, of glorious building in her honour, of the consummate artistry and rich humanity that burgeoned on every hand, I was so moved by the abundant beauty that I was almost healed of a wound that has ached in me all my life; the inferiority of women. It lamed me as a child. I still do not see why men feel such a need to stress it. Their behaviour seems unworthy, as though their superiority was not safe unless our inferiority was proven again and again. We are galled by it, even distorted by it, mortified for them, and forever puzzled. They have gifts and strengths we lack, achievement has been theirs, almost all concrete accomplishment is theirs, so why do they need to give us this flick of pain at our very being, we who are their mates and their mothers?

I was entranced by the Virgin whom Henry Adams deduced. She was loved, loved for her mercy, for her love of beauty and gift of inspiring its creation in others; loved above all for her generosity and power. She both gave and forgave. Then to honour the feminine enhances life. That is an arresting fact, often forgotten. But this great feminine symbol is a pattern that women do not follow, and could we? It is man's concept, and it is above all an appeal for mercy, and an appeal for bounty.

As long as men had this vision they could
project on to her the creative heights in their
own natures. They could represent their aspira-
tions and the profound depths of their being in
buildings that achieved miracles in stone, solving
mathematical problems of weight and balance
with the beauty of complete mastery.

It intoxicates, heals and shames me, and very
humbly I ask myself what relation can ordinary
women have to this divine feminine figure? Can
we, should we, even attempt to serve this vision?
We try to live her a little, we are expected to,
and that is a great honour. We would try to live
her more if we could, but the truth is we also
execrate, desecrate, and rail at her while we do
our chores. There is a smallness in us, a justified
resentment perhaps, that makes us tend to re-
duce life to chores as though to refute this great
ideal. It may be the contrast between the ideal
and the real that makes so many women hate
being women. Here we are caught, and here we
struggle.

The selfless, tireless one, the rich giver and

the meek receiver, with life-giving energy flow-
ing like milk from the breast, costing her nothing, is too, too much. Looked at in the grey light
of daily living the concept is the demand of the
ravening child, and we cannot respond to such a
claim in man or child. Our protest at the human
enactment of the ideal may be why we are not
worshipped, but belittled. Or is man's scorn a
cry for help, and one to be met? Does he need us
to be wiser than we are? He well might. Perhaps
life needs it too.

We do not often live with the superior side of
the man—that is generally expressed in his
work—but more habitually with his weak, tired,
shadow side. We indulge him, restore him, and
though we exploit him (that is a mutual game)
it often seems to us our role and fate to deal with
his inferiority, and conceal it from him. We may
do it with wisdom and grace, but usually we
project our faults onto each other, all can be
beneath comment, and there are times when
only mutual forgiveness makes us fit to face each
other once more.

Here is inferiority indeed, but it belongs to both and needs both to deal with it. It demands honesty and mercy, and these are not easy to summon; they may be beyond us, but when they answer our mutual cries of what can be despair, they are good enough to call divine. There can seem no connection between the great impersonal concepts and the problem of living our personal lives. Yet when men and women truly love each other they project their greatest possibilities onto the loved one. When love vanishes for a while the woman does not see the god in the man, he seldom lives it, and if he never sees the goddess in the woman it is never there.

Her failure may be the greater as she is the midwife of the profound forces stirred by love, and it is for her to join the ideal and the human, but she cannot do it alone. The intimacy that exists between men and women can seem the confrontation between good and evil, the place where there is the greatest chance of their being resolved by compassion and insight. It is here that souls are bared. Here in the welter of complete exposure we meet our glories and our sins, and we can see when we should have accused ourselves not the other: here too we may find the mutual support to enable us to say, "I see myself."

For small as we each can be we are more than our outer selves. Our potentialities, all those great forces that lie unconscious in our depths, accumulated through the ages, greater than we, mysterious to us, have to be represented to us in some outer form, in some person, in some concept, or we lose touch with them in ourselves, and live them feebly if at all. Or live destructively, which is worse.

Humanity apparently requires a concept of the superhuman in order to rise above the humdrum and the base within us. We need each other to see in seering truth what shame belongs to each, and what grace and goodness we receive from the other. And Oh—there are moments when our prayer to each other is—"Be my superior".

So I still care! At my age I care to my roots

about the quality of women, and I care because I know how important her quality is.

The hurt that women have borne so long may have immeasurable meaning. We women are the meeting place of the highest and the lowest, and of minutia and riches; it is for us to see, and understand, and have pride in representing ourselves truly. Perhaps we must say to man "You create us when you love us, but you destroy us both when you stress our inferiority. The time may have come for us to forge our own identity, dangerous as that will be."

Suddenly I see what I did not see before. I have felt all my life exactly as those feel who ask for equality. The real need is for honour, often not deserved, desired the more when not deserved. Our cry sounds as though we had been demeaned, and while we are demanding "Our rights" we are saying, "Do not demean us for our difference, self-shame is hard to bear."

106

The Measure of My Days

A letter has just come from a woman grieving over the weakness of character shown by her gifted husband. The secret inferiority of the man who in public is her superior can paralyse a woman's capacity to think, and make her refuse to feel. But human beings are not easily shattered. They continue to love, marry and wreck each other, in fact they dare to live. If they were not mostly blind to the effects of their behaviour how could the world go on?

If love unites opposites and overcomes law, then women have been given a role so great that it is strange we only sense it dimly. Was it clearer to us earlier, in the thirteenth century say when the Queen of Heaven reigned?

Easter Day

I am in that rare frame of mind when everything seems simple. When I have no doubt that the aim and solution of life is the acceptance of God. It is impossible and imperative, and clear. To open to such unimaginable greatness affrights my smallness. I do not know what I seek, cannot know, but I am where the mystery is the certainty.

My long life has hardly given me time—I cannot say to understand—but to be able to imagine that God speaks to me, says simply—"I keep calling to you, and you do not come", and I answer quite naturally—"I couldn't, until I knew there was nowhere else to go".

Perhaps our "No" to God is our sacred care. If our otherness matters, matters primarily, if we must fill our human role, represent the sacred tension, and say at the utmost point of our endurance and our yearning, "You are too different, you ask the impossible. Even at the cost of foregoing you altogether, it is our humanity that forces us to deny you. It was not only pride that made Lucifer oppose you. We too claim our right to a Luciferian 'No'. It has to be."

Then God might answer, "Of course that is your duty. If I had commanded anything less than the impossible, would you have recognized me as God?"

There being but one answer to that we remain silent and God adds, "This is what creation is. The might and marvel of forever creating out of opposition. Your blindness is almost strong enough to defeat me, but if the struggle were less would we belong together?"

*D*o *I know what I mean?* There is no notation to help one say these things, which both thought and feeling distort. But I must be as clear as I can. The experiences of the deep unconscious that came to me forty years ago were numinous, convincing proof of order and meaning in the universe. I knew I had a place in that order, and I felt contained. But not assured of protection or safety. Suffering was as likely as opportunity. Indeed suffering might be opportunity, or opportunity suffering. Logic and rightness generally lie too deep to see, chance can seem a near miracle, or the irony of life can show me how naturally I blunder, or how fortunate I am. Behind everything my conviction of meaning, as well as mystery, remains unchanged.

What do I mean by this new sense of simplicity, of it seeming clear that Christ was God and man, and that he symbolized the oneness in each of us? If oneness is what we seek that we may have roots to nourish us, at the same time knowing there is a division in that oneness, then where, where am I? It is not Job's acceptance of what was unfair because God was God. Is it that humanity has reached a place, perhaps a new place—how to say it—some words are too literal while others are so big that they sweep me into the air like balloons. I must stop generalizing. I, just I in my ignorance, would find satisfaction and relief in saying inside myself, at the dim, dumb point which is the best I can manage, there

The Measure of My Days

I feel impelled to say to God, "God and man have begun to seem like fellow creators. You created us, but we create you. Over and over again we create and recreate you as you are for us, and in us. It is our central task. We destroy you too, it is happening now, horribly. So that once again we have the terrifying task before us of creating you. It is happening everywhere, whether known or meant. You know all this, you may cause it in a way we cannot understand, but let me go on, let me be as clear to myself as I can. We are trying more and more to create ourselves, many think we can do it without you, but we are destroying ourselves too; we can't see our road, or ourselves, or you. Grant us this avowal, or recognition, yes recognition, as fellow creators, our small beside your great." No! It feels impious to claim, I can't go on.

I went and did some baking as it all seemed beyond me and I felt frightened. As I worked I saw that

The Measure of My Days

I had been rightly frightened, for I had thought it simple to say that God and man—in my childish, arrogant view—had become fellow creators, each of each; then as I remembered what man is making of himself I felt a sick recoil from humanity. But out of my need I assumed a myth that God had split himself in two, God and Lucifer, Heaven and Hell, and that this was so that consciousness could emerge. It was for man's sake, and the birth of man's insight. But as man attempts to stand alone, the split is more than he can endure and God is revealed as the power that binds us together. Man's independence has made the acknowledgement of God indispensable. On that let me rest.

In some central part of us mankind must always be trying to understand God. In that poignant core where we call out our questions, and cry for an answer. It is in each of us, even if question and answer are both despair. We are always talking

to God even while we argue him out of existence.
It is not easy to commune with that great force.
Can we do less than speak as creator to creator
since that seems the role given us, and in our
seeking we honour the honour done us.

I suppose this is what religion is about, and always
has been ever since man began to suffer and to
care why he suffered. I've taken a long time to
feel it as very truth. The last years may matter
most.

What frightens me is modern man's preference
for the arid. He claims to understand, yet knows
himself so little that he dares dispel mystery,
deny the depths of the human psyche, and prefers
to bypass the soul. It is inevitable that he arrives
in a desert without values. Life is being sterilized,
crime increases, and even children become

The Measure of My Days

murderers. It is as though God said, "You think to create order? Here is the appropriate disorder, since they are one".

In the midst of these contradictions something is stirring, something that feels like the beginning of a new pact. Man seems to be saying to the god within us, "Let us come closer. We know what we have been in your name, and we begin to see what we may be without you. We have begun to fear ourselves. We ask for recognition of a new thing in us. We are trying to extend our human understanding, to take on further responsibility for what we are. Help us to make a new image. If we have lost our fear of you, do not doubt our terror of ourselves. It is real."

As we face the god in us and come near our Luciferian sin, God may seem to die. If we cannot face this duality how are we to gain the mercy of inclusion that resolves all? I see now that it is so immeasurable a realization that it must always

seem new, always is new, for here God and man
are born afresh.

How can anyone conceive of a Godless world
without foreseeing our disintegration? Man's
first reaction to nature within him and outside
him must have been fear, awe, and the need of
meaning and value. What else have we been doing but searching for, insisting on, and creating
these as they tore us in two? We only survived
because we were searching for the power that
contained us.

If we are the meeting place of God and Satan, and
so it can feel, then without God we could become
Satan. If the God image should fade, vanish, we
could be left with our destroyer. We have been
devils of fanaticism in the name of God, and we
are now uncertain of the true name of the forces
within us. Am I struggling to say what man has
always been struggling to say, always and per-

haps forever and in every way, that it is man's chief role to define the difference between God and Satan? Each of us, lost and groping, begins to perceive it as our present task. It needs courage; Great God, grant us that.

The surgeon says I may pay my visit. I seem so well, so almost brilliantly well. I told the surgeon that it might be the last chance to see two of my grandchildren as they were leaving the country. He looked at me long and critically and said, "You may go". I am off, feeling almost drunk with health, shaky health. I have never had steady health, but better not to analyze. I am off, and I leave my note book behind. What need of a note book when one is out in the world?

It wasn't real. All that life in me was without a solid basis. Everyone spoke of my "newfound health" and said "I've never seen you like this before". So I paid two more visits, always cherished as a convalescent. I talked, how happily, and I walked with ease, though not far. For three weeks I lived at that height. Then I began to flag, I came home, and just petered out. Was I going to have a stroke? That dread thing in the back of every old head, that impairs and cruelly may not kill. I had severe headaches that went right down my spine, a numbness in my right arm and leg, strange symptoms unknown before, and I was spent, spent.

A GP came, a locum, and said, "Nervous exhaustion, and small wonder after all you've done, and at your age". I must rest; how I know that word, have known it all my life, so now I lie and rest. I rest even more than I always do. I must also "take exercise" so I drag myself out, my arthritic spine quickly fails me and I drag myself back as best I may. Anyone living alone, even in a small flat, takes constant exercise. Do doctors think you summon meals by magic, hot water bottles, all the things you think you might be more comfortable, or less uncomfortable, if you had, and have to get yourself? No one is more

The Measure of My Days

active, relatively, than the sick person who takes care of herself.

Now those worst ten days are over I improve hardly at all. The acute headache gone, a middle-sized one is always there. This is what is called taking things slowly. I do not exist, nor do I understand the ebb and flow of energy. I never have, and doctors understand it so little that they disregard it. Or truer to say they regard it as the patient's personal folly and no business of theirs. They may be right, and the patient longs to be equally superior but has to say, "It may not make sense, but it makes me!" As being too well brought me to the low place I now occupy I could curse my excessive reactions, but just because life is baffling it stirs one to artistry. It would clear my mind if I knew why a major operation at eighty-two stimulated me to an increase in vitality so convincing that now I have none.

I recoil from the idea that one must be compensated in another world for the hardness of this one. If this world is almost incomprehensible we are almost unteachable. Even tragedy barely makes us feel; its frequency may require the protection of not feeling, this is true, but thinking about tragedy barely affects our judgement. War follows war almost, not quite, as though no one had noticed the last war. Every aspect of tragedy must be the bones supporting the rest of life, the bravery, the drama and delights, and the calm, and all the small pleasures and beauties. What I cling to like a tool or a weapon in the hand of a man who knows how to use it, is the belief that difficulties are what makes it honourable and interesting to be alive.

I am uncertain whether it is a sad thing or a solace to be past change. One can improve one's character to the very end, and no one is too young in these days to put the old right. The late clarities will be put down to our credit I feel sure.

It was something other than this that had

caught my attention. In fact it was the exact opposite. It was the comfortable number of things about which we need no longer bother. I know I am thinking two ways at once, justified and possible in a note book. Goals and efforts of a lifetime can at last be abandoned. What a comfort. One's conscience? Toss the fussy thing aside. Rest, rest. So much over, so much hopeless, some delight remaining.

One's appearance, a lifetime of effort put into improving that, most of it ill judged. Only neatness is vital now, and one can finally live like a humble but watchful ghost. You need not plan holidays because you can't take them. You are past all action, all decision. In very truth the old are almost free, and if it is another way of saying that our lives are empty, well—there are days when emptiness is spacious, and non-existence elevating. When old, one has only one's soul as company. There are times when you can feel it crying, you do not ask why. Your eyes are dry, but heavy, hot tears drop on your heart. There is nothing to do but wait, and listen to the emptiness which is sometimes gentle. You and the day are quiet, and you have no comment to make.

I wish I could remember that Blake said, "Any fool can generalize". I generalize constantly. I write my notes as though I spoke for all old people. This is nonsense. Age must be different for each. We may each die from being ourselves. That small part that cannot be shared or shown, that part has an end of its own.

There is a word I have never found. It is a word for the thing most precious to man. Perhaps it is man's essence. Then why is there no right word for it? Pride, honour, both seem near, but they have too many aspects that are wrong. Soul comes near too, but it is seldom used in the way I mean. Perhaps we are still bringing the reality the word expresses into being, so we live it always but are not ready to name it. It is self-respect, but also the basis of self-respect. There is no reason why I should boggle at this phrase as though it did not say what is needed to be said, yet I must for it does not say enough.

The admonition "Have a proper respect for yourself" or "Your self-respect should have told you what to do" were both based on the assumption that you are of fine quality. It is this assumption that I want to name. Almost everyone makes the assumption; it can be a calamity when it is lacking. It is the assumption we used to live by, and we protect it so instinctively that we strike, even kill by reflex action if it is questioned.

Self-protection, self-preservation, these are words that ought to satisfy, but they do not seem to convey that passionate conviction that one can, and should, stand by what one is, but may not seem to be. No one must describe you truly with words that your reason would admit as accurate; you know you have done an unforgivable thing if you describe the acts of another truly. It is called disparagement, as though the bad thing was not a true statement. You may have stolen, but it is not right to call you a thief, and it is an insult that will not be borne, for you are more, more.

Who has the right to say what another is? It is here that I feel the conviction lies that we, the simplest and vaguest of us, know that we are other and better than we appear. More, that this is our basic assumption about ourselves. We put it to the test without a moment's reflection, attempting what we have never learned to do, dying with ease and style because we know there is greatness in us. It does not make our bad untrue; one is as poor a thing as one seems; but there is that in our being of which no man may speak ill.

If it is beyond naming, contradiction and confusion affecting it not at all, it is still man's point of passion, until I wonder if all the years we have been saying "self-respect" and "self-preservation" we spoke not of moral rectitude, or of physical preservation, but of what is descriptive of our true essence. We used "self" as it is used in the Upanishads, as the sacred identity within us, and to protect this is our chief aim.

It could be this, and we cannot name what we do not yet know.

After a time of trouble I found a likeable flat which was to be my home. I had had a long need of one, so it was also my dear shelter. My daughter and I moved in one evening with two suitcases, two beds, three pots of bulbs, a kettle and tea things. We lit a brilliant fire in the seemly little grate with the dry slats the builder had left after making a big opening between the two public rooms. I lay in the firelight peacefully listening to pigeons on the roof. To me pigeons say, "Too true, dear love, too true". I listened, looked out on trees beyond both windows and I was free and happy.

The flat had been repainted two months before but London dust sticks and the flat must be scrubbed. It was already so precious to me that its surface was almost my skin. A charwoman had been promised, and when next morning the bell of my flat pealed out I opened the door and there stood the most battered little figure I had ever seen. Only two yellow teeth, and hair almost burned away from a lifetime of curling tongs. I felt I could not invite her in, not into my dear, dear flat, but of course I did though feeling apologetic to the flat.

At the end of an hour's scrubbing she did some act of discrimination, of taste, I have forgotten what, and I exclaimed with pleasure and praised her rightness. She stopped scrubbing, drew herself to the full height of her weary little body and said slowly and graciously, "Our family has always been—different". I bowed my acknowledgement, she bowed her acceptance of my tribute, and the scrubbing went on.

That was many years ago, but only last year I passed a supermarket and saw coming out a slut of a woman. She was fat, unwashed, unkempt in hair and dress, with a large three-cornered tear in her overall. She looked large-hearted and vital, and as our eyes met something passed between us, we liked each other. She straightened up, placed one hand with fingers spread wide over the tear; then as we passed, we smiled seriously and bowed with equal dignity.

We know who we are even though we lack the precise name for it.

I never understood myself less. The humid summer makes me listless, age empties me, and this nervous exhaustion proves me truly spent. I feel profound lassitude, yet I am not ill. If someone comes and I talk I call up energy that I do not possess, and I may pay for it with an aching head lasting two or three days. I must talk less, I must become laconic. A smile, a nod, how unlikely, yet excessive talk must be based on vanity, an assumption that you are the fountain-head of interest. Age insists that I be dull as a further disability. No one else will mind, perhaps not even notice. Others might prefer me silent. I will try.

I may be gaining strength. I do not know. I

do know that to assure someone I am better creates a hole that used to be filled by the energy used up in saying I am better.

Today I must be better for I suffer, and it gives me energy. I have lost some of my lassitude for I am angry, angry at sorrow, at the impossibility of expressing it. Life is so many-sided that nothing can be clearly put. One is left throbbing with it so no wonder one is angry, though not with anyone, just hot with protest. Anger must be the energy that has not yet found its right channel.

I accept the reasonableness of the event that pains me. I see its necessity, but my heart is a storm of loss. I am part of my family as they sail down the channel only a few miles away at this moment. I am happy with them, thrilled with them, I feel the excitement of the children, the pleasure of their father as he shows them the great ship. I feel the wind blowing, I feel everyone astir with the sense of the long voyage ahead.

The Measure of My Days

I have all this clear in my head, but at the same time I suffer at their going. I am bereft. And I am angry that nothing can be said, I can't keen my woe, and I can't tell my love, and I hate the outrage we do ourselves in that we have no forms to convey feeling. It is a lie to be cheerful, and so I am left with this passion with which I can do nothing.

If I liked the actual physical presence of people more I might not love their essence so much. The precious quality in them that appears and disappears, that ennobles the features, sweetens the eyes for a radiant instant, that makes a sensitive boy ignite with interest, or a man standing silently by the fire strengthen my heart. I am losing contact with their dearness. I can treasure them in my memory, feel the wound of difference, flush with affection, but the ship is taking them out of my life. They will change, I will fade in their minds, and I will no longer see them live their lives. The pain of love, the sheer pain of it.

I wonder why pain brings energy. Six years ago I had the fractured femur, and felt energy come to me, new energy, and knew I was stronger than I had been before the accident; it is again like that. The same happened with the major operation, and now with the pain of parting I am more alive, and I protest that no form of expression accompanies this energy. This love and pain and energy that are so strong while I am so weak, what do I do with them? I could bear them better if I could play an organ and let everything in me roll and rumble out in a great volume of sound. No, that would not help, I need to be the organ and compose out of my own being.

Now, have I found what I want? Is there an idea near at hand that will help? I feel it, but I cannot yet think it. It is the possibility that all intense experience is an increase of energy. It is the intensity of being that turns us into prisms, we split consciousness into qualities and we have to endure the passion of doing this. We cannot express it for we are the process. The problem is not what we do with it but enduring what it does to us.

The Measure of My Days

Daily, hourly we must keep the crystal clear that the colours may assume their order. I pray to fulfil my task, don't elude me now for my soul's sake. I must live so that clarity produces the order of diversity. Nothing less than bearing it all will do, for it is the creation of a change of consciousness. Nothing less, and no words are needed. It is the mystery that is done to us; as though love and pain and emergence are all intensified energy by which one is fired, ordered and perhaps annealed. The purpose of life may be to clarify our essence, and everything else is the rich, dull, hard, absorbing chaos that allows the central transmutation. It is unstatable, divine and enough.

I feel people moving like patterns I cannot decipher, and I ask all those who like me seem to do nothing:" Does the passion in our hearts somehow serve?".

Again a day that is so empty that I cry inside, a heavy weeping that will not stop. I cannot read, the papers depress me, reviews are written from points of view so outside my experience that I wonder if I ever understood anything. The grey sky seems very grey, but I finally soothe myself by small duties, putting away freshly ironed linen, watering plants. Order, cleanliness, seemliness make a structure that is half support, half ritual, and if it does not create it maintains decency. I make my possessions appear at their best as they are my only companions. Some days it is the only improvement I can bring about. I remember a beautiful girl of seventeen with destructive parents; unable to improve her position in any way she burst out with the surprising phrase, "I could neaten the stars". With less need I neaten my flat.

Old people can seldom say "we"; not those who live alone, and even those who live with their families are alone in their experience of age, so the habit of thinking in terms of "we" goes, and they become "I". It takes increasing courage to be "I" as one's frailty increases. There is so little strength left that one wants shelter, one seeks the small and natural, but where to find it?

A garden, a cat, a wood fire, the country, to walk in woods and fields, even to look at them, but these would take strength I have not got, or a man whom also I have not got. So, here in a flat, I must make the round of the day pleasant, getting up, going to bed, meals, letters with my breakfast tray: can I make it total to a quiet heart? I have to be a miracle of quiet to make the flame in my heart burn low, and on some good days I am a miracle of quiet. But I cannot conceive how age and tranquillity came to be synonymous.

For days I have been unwilling to record my distress caused by the degree of organization we must expect in the future. I am on my third book which tells of a society so planned that the individual as we conceive him would disappear. Such a world is imperative it seems, already far advanced, and nothing can stop it. Industry finds it necessary, the increase in population makes it obligatory, and communism and capitalism are meaningless terms for societies becoming more and more alike.

The basic concept of oneness has undergone a great change. It no longer lends us greatness. It now reduces us for it is the practical problem of providing for the many. But this may change the very core of our being. Is it that the concept of oneness used to be carried by our image of God, and now the sense of an all-creating, all-containing power has gone? If we are bereft of all sense of a spiritual force arousing our awe, granting us value, instilling us with fear of ourselves and our fate, do we now seek some other greatness in which to lose ourselves? Do we will to be contained, and protected from life's polarity?

Has the conception of oneness been projected onto the outside world? If it is no longer centred in God giving us each a source where we are greater than ourselves, are we empty, almost

meaningless? Where we used to pray to be serv-
ants of one God, we now ask to be organized
into a whole, and we have already begun to
worship, and to fear, that whole. Then is it we
who force the able minds to answer our needs?
Can one surmise what will follow? We know that
the unconscious compensates the conscious, so if
we create a world of contained units, conforming,
agreeing, adapting that all parts may fit the
whole, what will then arise in the unconscious of
each? If automatically we conform, violence
could arise as counterpole.

Tranquil? The old tranquil? I am leaden with
foreboding. Not for myself. For human-kind,
which isn't in my care.

These books have lamed me. Can one not trust to
the richly gifted men and women to keep life
varied and creative? It would seem so, yet within
one or two generations standards may have

undergone a complete change, and conforming would have become morality. Or a static society could arouse the individual to passionate protest, and criticism, and a very flowering of needed individuality might take place. Yet if we are entering an age of numbers, to differ could become a social sin, endangering the good of all, and such a system might last for ages. Could the very irrationality of life not be trusted to defeat this chimera of the intellect? That it fascinates good and less good minds is certain, that it has wounded me for weeks shows that I am too old to expose myself to speculation. I feel aged by it all, aged.

There is self-pity and rancour in the old, in me. It is partly the demand of the child for safety supplied by someone else. I am failing, modernity is frightening, the old can barely keep a steady stance, so may our cries be forgiven us.

Yesterday I finished my fourth book on the inevitability of a planned world. No mention was made of the high calibre of the people who would be required to create world order, and nothing less was expected. Nor was the temptation to tyranny dealt with. Today I recalled the difficulty always experienced in making people do what it is thought they ought to do, even with the most severe methods tried, and my hopes rose a little.

I thought of great plans failing everywhere, of mighty America ineffectually trying to impose her will, of the plight of England, and I now felt more able to face the frightening fertility of man's mind. His abstract ideas, extreme, inhuman, and from which we are only saved by the incalculable turns of life itself. What a boon disparity is—difference of opinion has never been sufficiently appreciated. It is the unexpected, the unknowable, the divine irrationality of life that saves us.

But I also remember a fellow passenger who had made twenty-five trips between Australia and Europe. After four weeks at sea she asked me if I was enjoying the trip. I said that I did not really like shipboard life, but the sea was a mighty experience. She nodded in agreement, saying, "I've spent weeks on it, and I've seen it again and again from the air. It's a great sight. You know all the ideas men have, how they're always talking about something like the world being round, and so on. Well, I give it to them. From the air the earth looks round. They may know what they're talking about more often than we think".

We old people are not in modern life. Our impressions of it are at second or third hand. It is something we cannot know. We do know its effect on us, and the impact is so great that it can alienate us from our past, making it seem un-

The Measure of My Days

likely and irrelevant. We live in a limbo of our
own. Our world narrows, its steady narrowing
is a constant pain. Friends die, others move
away, some become too frail to receive us, and
I become too frail to travel to them. Talk ex-
hausts us, the expense of the telephone reduces
us to a breathless rush of words, so that letters
are our chief channel of friendship. Letters can
be scarce so we tend to live in a world of our own
making, citizens of Age, but otherwise stateless.

*T*he old are unsure of a future, their past has
grown stale so they are dependent on the sentience of the moment. It behoves us to be sentient.

Or—the old live by recalling the past, and are
fascinated by the query of what future is possible.
Their present is empty.

Or—there is nothing of interest to be said
about the old, except that they are absorbed by
age.

Each could be true. One takes one's choice.

I don't like to write this down, yet it is much in the minds of the old. We wonder how much older we have to become, and what degree of decay we may have to endure. We keep whispering to ourselves, "Is this age yet? How far must I go?". For age can be dreaded more than death. "How many years of vacuity? To what degree of deterioration must I advance?" Some want death now, as release from old age, some say they will accept death willingly, but in a few years. I feel the solemnity of death, and the possibility of some form of continuity. Death feels a friend because it will release us from the deterioration of which we cannot see the end. It is waiting for death that wears us down, and the distaste for what we may become.

These thoughts are with us always, and in our hearts we know ignominy as well as dignity. We are people to whom something important is about to happen. But before then, these endless years before the end, can we summon enough merit to warrant a place for ourselves? We go into the future not knowing the answer to our question.

But we also find that as we age we are more alive than seems likely, convenient, or even bearable. Too often our problem is the fervour of life within us. My dear fellow octogenarians, how are we to carry so much life, and what are we to do with it?

Let no one say it is "unlived life" with any of the simpler psychological certitudes. No one lives all the life of which he was capable. The unlived life in each of us must be the future of humanity. When truly old, too frail to use the vigour that pulses in us, and weary, sometimes even scornful of what can seem the pointless activity of mankind, we may sink down to some deeper level and find a new supply of life that amazes us.

All is uncharted and uncertain, we seem to lead the way into the unknown. It can feel as though all our lives we have been caught in absurdly small personalities and circumstances and beliefs. Our accustomed shell cracks here, cracks there, and that tiresomely rigid person we supposed to be ourselves stretches, expands, and with all inhibitions gone we realize that age is not failure, nor disgrace; though mortifying we did not invent it. Age forces us to deal with idleness, emptiness, not being needed, not able to do, helplessness just ahead perhaps. All this is true, but one has had one's life, one could be full to the brim. Yet it is the end of our procession through time, and our steps are uncertain.

Here we come to a new place of which I knew nothing. We come to where age is boring, one's interest in it by-passed; further on, go further on, one finds that one has arrived at a larger place still, the place of release. There one says, "Age can seem a debacle, a rout of all one most needs, but that is not the whole truth. What of the part of us, the nameless, boundless part who experienced the rout, the witness who saw so much go, who remains undaunted and knows with clear conviction that there is more to us than age?

Part of that which is outside age has been created
by age, so there is gain as well as loss. If we have
suffered defeat we are somewhere, somehow
beyond the battle".

Now that I am sure this freedom is the right
garnering of age I am so busy being old that I
dread interruptions. This sense of vigour and
spaciousness may cease, and I must enjoy it
while it is here. It makes me feel, "I serve life,
certain that it is the human soul that discerns the
spirit, and that we are creators". But victims
too. Life happens to us. Plan and try as we will,
think, believe, it is still that inscrutable mood of
the time that casts the die. We suffer as we
change, that life may change in us. We also
destroy, and the pain that for me is inherent in
life is that we do not know when we create and
when we destroy. That is our incurable blindness, but perhaps we are less dangerous if we
know we do not see.

A long life makes me feel nearer truth, yet it won't go into words, so how can I convey it? I can't, and I want to. I want to tell people approaching and perhaps fearing age that it is a time of discovery. If they say—"Of what?" I can only answer, "We must each find out for ourselves, otherwise it won't be discovery". I want to say—"If at the end of your life you have only yourself, it is much. Look, you will find".

I would like to be as outspoken as old people feel, but honesty gives pain. Few enjoy honesty for it arouses feeling, and to avoid the pain of feeling many prefer to live behind steel doors. It is not being able to say conflicting things with one breath that is the sad division between human beings. As some dislike the paradoxical we forego the fun of admitting what we know, and so miss the entertainment of being mutually implicated in truth.

One cannot be honest even at the end of one's life, for no one is wholly alone. We are bound to those we love, or to those who love us, and to those who need us to be brave, or content, or even happy enough to allow them not to worry about us. So we must refrain from giving pain, as our last gift to our fellows. For love of humanity consume as much of your travail as you can. Not all, never that terrible muteness that drains away human warmth. But when we are almost free of life we must retain guile that those still caught in life may not suffer more. The old must often try to be silent, if it is within their power, since silence may be like space, the intensely alive something that contains all. The clear echo of what we refrained from saying, everything, from the first pause of understanding, to the quiet of comprehension.

After weeks of not writing in my note book I took it up again, and some change had taken place. A sense of naturalness has come, or of freedom. Is a sense of the naturalness of being old tranquillity? Then the old can be tranquil, but it is an achievement. If at the end we choose to represent tranquillity, as without us it might be missing, let it be clearly seen that tranquillity is not a grace waiting for us to take on as our right, but something we have to win with effort. It may not be our doing. It may be what facing age does to us. Then here lies our victory.

Man is truly astonishing. One would imagine his basic belief would be that struggle is natural and inevitable. I have supposed that the rock on which we all stood was that life was almost more than we could manage. But man's history has much of the surprising in it, and it is now clear to me that from the beginning some human beings saw that the best way of taking life was lightly. Undeterred by what happened to him and to others, man has had a genius for ease. To be so unaffected by reality is inspiring.

I could understand his slowly but surely seeing that his own behaviour was the one thing it was within his power to control, somewhat, but he tossed this aside to be caught by those handicapped from birth with a conscience. He had no difficulty in avoiding that monolith that I assumed lay on the path of each, the granite fact that though life thwarted him at every turn it did ennoble his character. Only a few gloomy people saw this. The hordes of the ages with wits sharpened by experience rushed to get what was desirable, leaving to others what was difficult, even inventing the idea of duty to slow them up, while he reached ease quickly since to enjoy life was his true inheritance.

Early, very early on, there were those who claimed ease as their own, and who knew what to do with it. I have proof of this, and I got it at the zoo.

I was watching a young female monkey swinging from the top bar of her cage. She was pregnant and interested me. She turned, caught my appraising eye, and swinging gracefully down sat in the straw on the floor of the cage. Then with languid elegance she drew the straw waist high, as though it had been a carriage rug, casting on me so withering a glance that I withdrew with silent apologies. I remembered such glances cast on me from the occupants of great cars, if I stood on the curbstone waiting for them to pass, possibly in the rain. Yes, and I had felt in my own eye that sidelong look of unconcern when it was I who happened to be in a car.

Belief in ease began a long way back, and was part of life from the beginning. The skill of being effortless is part of life. As I regard it with the astonishment it deserves I no longer ask myself how it ever entered the human brain that you ought to have what you want, for I accept that it did, and that this is one of man's many triumphs.

I continue to be spellbound by ease for I recall a visit to a music hall some fifty years ago. A stout, knowing man, wearing his topper at an angle, strolled onto the stage lazily swinging a stick. He nodded intimately to distant points in the audience, and sang a song with sophisticated good nature that won him affectionate applause. Then he sang the same song silently; at moments moving his lips, giving a half twirl to his stick, lifting a finger as accent, living the rhythm with exquisite accuracy, and masterly indifference. When the song was finished his pleasure broke into a grin, and the audience roared its appreciation. They stamped feet, beat hands, their noisy admiration burst into a frenzy over the man who dared to be so unconcerned.

I too felt immeasurably relaxed.

Conversation must be near the top of human pleasures. Babies, even a few months old, have discovered this, and beguile themselves with what sounds like reflective conversation. They modulate sounds thoughtfully and subtly, in fact they enthrall themselves with the comfort of the human voice, as satisfying when alone as with a companion. If my youngest grandchild, at eight months, pauses as though he had offered all his observations for the time being, I say something like, "But there must have been more to it than that", and he then continues as though he had indeed recalled another aspect of the subject.

The sound of speech and pausing for a friend to contribute sound is one of the earliest needs. Sleep would come first, then food, protest perhaps third, then the pleasure in showing happiness and affection, and speech as the fifth solid satisfaction.

Silence receives too little appreciation, silence being a higher, rarer thing than sound. Silence implies inner riches, and a savouring of impressions. Babies value this too. They lie silent, and one can suppose them asleep, but look closer, and with eyes wide open they are sparkling like jewels in the dark. Silence is beyond many of us, and hardly taken into account as one of life's favours. It can be sacred. Its implications are unstatable. It has a superiority that makes the interruption of the spoken word crude, rendering small what was infinite.

The Measure of My Days

My youngest grandchild uses silence as well as he does sound. He is consummate in making soft, confiding noises that bind the heart of the hearer to him. But for long periods he prefers to keep his own counsel. Then he looks forth on the world unblinking, unhurried, and with a dignity that should be the rite of Kings.

At times he gazes at me without interest; above self-doubt he yawns, a wide, slow, complete and uncovered yawn. He removes his gaze from me so that I wonder if I was seen, if I was present. With grave deliberation he discovers a hole in the arm of his chair so small that no one else could have had the calm to take it in, and he gives it his undivided attention. He gives all of himself to that hole which just fits the tip of his minute first finger, and I know that all hope of further conversation with him is over. I also know that I have been in the presence of perfect naturalness, and I feel chastened and uplifted.

Our earth began with fire, achieved water, and grew its infinite variety of vegetation. Animals evolved in a fantasia of form. Man struggled to consciousness, possessed imagination, endured self-awareness, and experienced the spirit within him. Can we do less than give fealty to such ascension?